"Loftin and Leyf have succeeded in writing precisely the introduction I wish had existed when I began my own studies of Barfield's thought. This will be a helpful text for newcomers as well as veteran Barfieldians still struggling with difficult distinctions between alpha- and beta-thinking or original and final participation. Interest in Barfield has surged over the past decade, and this timely volume represents one of the best attempts to stand (as Barfield says of Coleridge) 'inside' his thought rather than '*beside*' it."

—JAKE GREFENSTETTE, University of Cambridge

What Barfield Thought

What Barfield Thought

AN INTRODUCTION TO THE WORK OF OWEN BARFIELD

LANDON LOFTIN
MAX LEYF

CASCADE *Books* · Eugene, Oregon

WHAT BARFIELD THOUGHT
An Introduction to the Work of Owen Barfield

Cascade Books
An Imprint of Wipf and Stock Publishers
199 W. 8th Ave., Suite 3
Eugene, OR 97401

www.wipfandstock.com

PAPERBACK ISBN: 978-1-6667-3676-2
HARDCOVER ISBN: 978-1-6667-9554-7
EBOOK ISBN: 978-1-6667-9555-4

Cataloguing-in-Publication data:

Names: Loftin, Landon, author. | Leyf, Max, author.

Title: What Barfield Thought : An Introduction to the Work of Owen Barfield / Landon Loftin and Max Leyf.

Description: Eugene, OR: Cascade Books, 2023 | Includes bibliographical references and index.

Identifiers: ISBN 978-1-6667-3676-2 (paperback) | ISBN 978-1-6667-9554-7 (hardcover) | ISBN 978-1-6667-9555-4 (ebook)

Subjects: LCSH: Barfield, Owen, 1898–1997. | English literature—20th century—History and criticism. | Imagination.

Classification: BR117 .W37 2023 (paperback) | BR117 (ebook)

04/28/23

Contents

Acknowledgments

LANDON LOFTIN AND MAX LEYF,
WHAT BARFIELD THOUGHT

I (LANDON) WOULD LIKE to thank my family, especially my parents and my wife, Kate; they have all, in one way or another, encouraged me to pursue my sometimes eccentric interests. Additionally, I would like to thank those who have helped me in the process of writing this book: Edward Stengel, Zach Manis, Steven Kurtz, Matthew Bradt, John Hanel, and Jacob Krato. Thanks are also due to Stephen Thorson and Jake Gefenstette for providing helpful comments on the manuscript. Finally, I would like to thank the editorial staff at the Wade Center for their help on an article, which has been revised for use in this book, and for their gracious permission to draw from that material in chapter 5.

I (MAX) WOULD LIKE to thank, foremost, my collaborator *sine qua non*, Landon, for his initiative in setting up this project, his diligence in seeing it through to its completion, and his patience with the dilatory approach that his colleague sometimes assumed in respect to the latter's appointed tasks. I also wish to acknowledge sustained appreciation for Barfield's lifelong dedication to the work which has served as the subject of this book and this is perhaps as good a place as any to express this.

FINALLY, TOGETHER WE WOULD like to thank Owen A. Barfield for everything he has done to encourage and enable this and other attempts to illuminate the life and thought of his grandfather.

Introduction

As interest in Owen Barfield grows, we aim to meet the need for a scholarly introduction to his thought. Our primary purpose is to present an overview, analysis, and synthesis of Barfield's most salient ideas in a manner that will be of interest to neophytes and initiates alike. Barfield's work can, at times, be difficult to understand; C. S. Lewis put it well when he described Barfield's style of argument as "dark, labyrinthine," and "pertinacious."[1] But Lewis ardently promoted Barfield's work because he knew that people who willingly walk in those dim and winding corridors are, in time, richly rewarded by the bright light at their end. We offer the present work in service to those who wish to undertake this adventure.

While the present book will help those readers who wish to engage Barfield for the sake of achieving a greater understanding of and appreciation for other writers who have been associated with or influenced by him, we aim first and foremost to present Barfield as a profound and original thinker in his own right. Regrettably, Barfield's place in history has largely been determined by his relation to other figures—most notably, to C. S. Lewis and the other Inklings, as well as Samuel Taylor Coleridge and Rudolf Steiner. Without intending to detract from the significance of any of these thinkers, we argue that the time has come for Barfield's work to emerge from the shadows of other works and to take its place in the sun.

In 1971, Barfield published a book called *What Coleridge Thought*, which takes an approach to the work of Samuel Taylor Coleridge that will, in some respects, serve as a model for our treatment of Barfield. In *What Coleridge Thought*, Barfield observed that, although Coleridge is now mostly remembered for his poetry, there was a time when he was known primarily for his contributions to philosophy.[2] *What Coleridge Thought*

1. Quoted from Harwood, *C. S. Lewis, My Godfather*, 28.
2. Barfield includes a remarkable quote from John Stuart Mill to substantiate the

1

was therefore intended to fan the dying embers of Coleridge's reputation as a philosopher. Barfield noted in his introduction that prior treatments of Coleridge's philosophy had been largely characterized by what he deemed "the comparative approach," which, though potentially interesting and useful in its own way, entails certain limitations. For instance: "A student . . . who picks up a contemporary book on Coleridge, in order to find what he thought about things, is likely to find himself involved in a complex and allusive web of comparative philosophy." Additionally, and more relevant to our purposes, Barfield maintained that the comparative approach imposes crucial limitations on the author: "[I]t keeps him too much outside of the intellectual content with which he is dealing."[3] To make this point more forcefully, with specific reference to prior treatments of Coleridge, Barfield quoted J. A. Appleyard:

> What is wanting in the sizable bibliography of literature on Coleridge is a full-scale study of the development of his philosophy which will consider him on his own terms and not as a representative of something else, whether it be German idealism, English Platonism, pantheistic mysticism, semantic analysis, or depth psychology. The idea or organizing insight ought to be internal to his thought, so as to see what that thought is and not merely what it is like or unlike.[4]

While we will engage in a fair amount of comparative philosophizing—some of it, of necessity, being rather "complex and allusive"—our aim is to treat Barfield "on his own terms and not as a representative of something else." This, rather than the purely comparative approach, is what we understand to be the best way to proceed with an introductory text. References to other thinkers or schools of thought, therefore, will be made insofar as they shed light on Barfield, but it is our conviction that one reason why Barfield has so often been misunderstood and (more often) ignored is *because* he cannot neatly be fit into recognized categories. He was far too original to be treated as a mere representative of, or supplement to, something or someone else. This is true even in reference to the thinkers who most influenced him, like Rudolf Steiner. And though his contributions to anthroposophy and his

---

point: "Bentham excepted, no Englishman of recent date has left his impress so deeply on the opinions and mental tendencies of those among us who attempt to enlighten their practice by philosophical meditation." *What Coleridge Thought*, 1.

3. Barfield, *What Coleridge Thought*, 2.

4. Barfield, *What Coleridge Thought*, 3. Barfield quoted this passage from Appleyard's *Coleridge's Philosophy of Literature*.

membership in the Oxford Inklings are very important, Barfield must not be treated simply as an adjunct to either.

One needs only a passing familiarity with Barfield's work to guess with confidence what "idea or organizing insight" we will be using to expound Barfield's philosophy: it is, of course, *the evolution of consciousness*. To offer a provisional definition of the term that it will be, in large part, the purpose of the chapters to follow to flesh out, the evolution of consciousness is a theory that posits a process of fundamental change in relation between the human mind and the material world, affecting not only how people have perceived and understood the world, but also the fundamental character of that which is perceived (i.e., the world itself). This change involves, among other things, a movement from the conscious participation in the life of nature characteristic of pre-modern consciousness to the self-conscious observation of nature that characterizes modern consciousness.[5] This idea and its implications will be developed from a number of different angles in the coming chapters. For this reason, we wish here only to offer a few preliminary remarks to orient our readers and circumvent some possible misunderstandings. These misunderstandings come, first and foremost, from a failure to firmly grasp the distinction between what Barfield means by "the evolution of consciousness," on one hand, and what is ordinarily meant by "the history of ideas," on the other.

Inquiry into the history of ideas, according to Barfield, is often pursued in something like the following manner:

> [I]nstead of wrestling, head on, with—let us say—the philosophy of Aristotle, and asking where he was right and where he was wrong, we trace how the ideas that constitute that philosophy arose as corrections, modifications, refutations of the philosophy of Plato and the pre-Socratics before him; and then we observe how those ideas were themselves corrected, modified, refuted by later thinkers; we arrive by that route at the Scholastic philosophers of the Middle Ages, and by the like dialectical

---

5. Here and elsewhere we use the term "modern" in accordance with Barfield's usage, which simply designates the epoch inaugurated by the Scientific Revolution. Additionally, we have used "postmodern" in its broadest sense: the current epoch in which many of the assumptions that are distinctive of modernity are being called into question. Certain reservations must, of course, be expressed. Modernity is here characterized as an era defined by certain assumptions and tendencies. This is not to suggest that there have been no individuals or groups within the modern era that have resisted—some with admirable success—the process by which distinctively modern assumptions and tendencies became dominant in the West. Additionally, there have been significant counter-movements such as Romanticism, Transcendentalism, and, of particular importance to Barfield, Anthroposophy.

progression on to Francis Bacon, Descartes, the English Empiri-
cists, Kant and so forth.[6]

Such a study of the history of philosophy (or the history of any other field
of inquiry) can be interesting and useful insofar as it is not conducted under
the naïve assumption that "all these philosophers were asking themselves the
same questions and finding different answers to them; that they were talking about the same things, and merely reasoning differently about them."[7]
Unfortunately, despite the fact this assumption is often rejected in theory, it
is just as often affirmed in practice. The result of this, Barfield said, is the all
too common mistake of treating the history of philosophy "as though it were
a dialogue between contemporaries."[8] Barfield's criticism, then, is not aimed
at the history of ideas *per se*, but rather at those who write and speak about
the history of ideas as if the process by which important historical thinkers
have reached their conclusions has been wholly dialectical—in his words,
"that the thread on which [their conclusions] are strung is dialectical only."[9]

On the surface, this critique sounds similar to one that many other
scholars have leveled against the assumptions behind much that has been
written about the history of ideas. For instance, Alasdair MacIntyre, speaking particularly of moral philosophy, bemoans the "persistently unhistorical
treatment of the subject":

> We all too often still treat the moral philosophers of the past
> as contributors to a single debate with a relatively unvarying
> subject-matter, treating Plato and Hume and Mill as contempo-
> raries both of ourselves and of each other.... This leads to an ab-
> straction of these writers from the cultural and social milieus in
> which they lived and thought and so the history of their thought
> acquires a false independence from the rest of the culture.[10]

Thus, he says that "Kant ceases to be part of the history of Prussia, Hume
is no longer a Scotsman. For from the standpoint of [philosophy] as we
conceive it these characteristics have become irrelevancies."[11] Admirable as
it is, however, MacIntyre's sensitivity to historical and cultural context is not
itself what Barfield has in mind. Barfield's primary concern was for differences of *consciousness* between people in different places and times. These

6. Barfield, *History, Guilt, and Habit*, 3–4.

7. Barfield, *History, Guilt, and Habit*, 4.

8. Barfield, *History, Guilt, and Habit*, 4.

9. Barfield, *History, Guilt, and Habit*, 4.

10. MacIntyre, *After Virtue*, 12–13.

11. Barfield, *History, Guilt, and Habit*, 4.

differences in consciousness often correlate with differences in historical and cultural context, but are not reducible to them.

In order to get the crux of the distinction between the evolution of consciousness and the history of ideas, it is necessary to spend some time clarifying what Barfield means by the complex and multivalent term "consciousness." Again, much of this analysis and clarification will come *en route* as the book progresses, but a few more preliminary remarks will here be offered on the following questions: What does Barfield mean by "consciousness"? What does it mean to say that consciousness *changes* or evolves? And in what sense do changes in consciousness correlate to changes in the world?

The term "consciousness" is most commonly used to designate the mere fact of a creature's awareness of itself or its surroundings, but this renders it indistinguishable from the term "sentience" and, moreover, it is not the primary sense in which Barfield uses it.[12] The evolution of consciousness is not, therefore, a theory put forward in contribution to the well-established and ongoing debate about whether and how biological evolution, by means of natural selection, could have brought about creatures with simple awareness and a first-person perspective.[13] Barfield anticipated that the word "consciousness" would cause this sort of confusion, but he found no better alternative in English. He once suggested that his meaning was closer to what is meant by *weltanschauung* in German, which is commonly translated into English (with the risk of considerable semantic dilution) as "worldview." Nevertheless, Barfield chose to use the term consciousness instead of its German alternative because even *weltanschauung* failed to convey his meaning. He expressed his resignation as follows:

> If . . . the word *consciousness* is taken not simply in its finite sense, as "the opposite of unconsciousness," but rather as including a man's whole awareness of his environment, the sum total of his intellectual and emotional experiences as an individual, perhaps it may serve.[14]

In other words, Barfield was not primarily concerned with the mere fact of consciousness, but with its fundamental character, which determines not

12. "Verbally and logically 'conscious' and 'unconscious' are contradictories, but we do not use them in that way. When we say 'the unconscious,' we do not simply mean 'the non-conscious.'" Barfield, "Dream, Myth and Philosophical Double-Vision," *Rediscovery of Meaning and Other Essays*, 30.

13. Those interested in the difficulties inherent in the thesis that biological evolution alone has produced creatures with a first-person perspective (which is separate from, but not entirely unrelated to Barfield's theory) should see the chapter on consciousness in Thomas Nagel's *Mind and Cosmos*, 35–70.

14. Barfield, *History in English Words*, 86.

whether, but *how* a person perceives the world, and defines the limits within which they are prone to think and feel.

This sense of the word "consciousness" is elsewhere used, for example, by translators of H. G. Gadamer, who wrote, in a passage that sums up the radical insight that seems to follow from drawing a sharp distinction between the history of ideas and the evolution of consciousness, that "It is part of the elementary experience of philosophy that when we try to understand the classics of philosophical thought, they of themselves make a claim to truth that the consciousness of later times can neither reject nor transcend."[15] Without overstating the similarities between Barfield and Gadamer, we can say they share at least this much in common: the differences in consciousness between people who are far removed from each other in space and time are often, at least to some degree, *incommensurable.*

A few reservations must be noted about the idea of "incommensurability." First of all, it will evoke in many readers an association with the concept of a "paradigm" as defined in Thomas Kuhn's *The Structure of Scientific Revolutions.*[16] There is a fruitful comparison here, but it must be borne in mind that the scope of Barfield's concern includes scientific paradigms, but is not limited to them. The revolution of paradigms, which Kuhn identified as the best way to understand the nature of scientific progress, is closely bound up with the way in which consciousness changes over the course of history. At the same time, however, paradigm shifts as Kuhn describes them can be understood in terms of the history of ideas, whereas Barfield's thesis can only be grasped in terms of an evolution in consciousness. This is to say that, to understand Barfield's work, it is necessary to conceive of the substrate in which paradigms of knowledge (scientific or otherwise) are rooted. More will be said of this in chapter 5.

An additional difficulty that talk of incommensurability may present is that it suggests that ancient modes of consciousness are inaccessible to contemporary people. Barfield is, in fact, quite sanguine about the prospect of bridging differences in consciousness. In other words, the incommensurability between modes of consciousness, insofar as it attains in a given

15. Gadamer, *Truth and Method,* xxi. It is worth pointing out that what Barfield meant by "consciousness" is actually most fully expressed by Gadamer in his conception of a "horizon," which he defined as "The totality of all that can be realised or thought about by a person at a given time in history and in a particular culture." *Philosophical Hermeneutics,* 305.

16. Kuhn, *Structure of Scientific Revolutions, passim.* Barfield anticipated a fair amount that Kuhn wrote, and spoke approvingly of his work. One obvious difference between Kuhn and Barfield is that Kuhn was led by his investigations into the history of science to an anti-realist conception of truth; Barfield, on the other hand, shared a robust, though nuanced, realism with C. S. Lewis.

situation, is surmountable, though usually not without great effort. Barfield was confident in the power of the imagination, properly cultivated and trained, to enter into other, usually older, states of consciousness. Indeed, he persistently argues that the future intellectual competence and spiritual health of humanity depends on our willingness to do so.

Finally, it is worth introducing Barfield's firm belief that it is a mistake to assume that the study of consciousness is only concerned with changes in the subjective, inner world of human experience. If this were true, the historical study of consciousness would really be reducible, if not to a simple history of ideas, at least to something better described as the evolution of human psychology. But Barfield's theory is not addressed (or, at least not primarily addressed) to the evolution of human psychology. For Barfield, while the inner world of consciousness may be distinguished from the outer world of nature, it cannot be divided from it.[17] This is because "nature" (a term that Barfield often used in its older sense to denote the whole of the phenomenal world) is what it is largely by virtue of the fact that it is participated by consciousness (see chapter 4 for more on the nature of "participation"). What is important to note here is simply that Barfield believed that the study of consciousness and the changes that it has undergone are inseparable from the study of nature and *vice versa*. When it comes to consciousness, Barfield argues,

> We are not studying some so-called "inner" world, divided off by a skin or a skull, from a so-called "outer" world; we are trying to study the world itself from its inner aspect. Consciousness is not a tiny bit of the world stuck on to the rest of it. It is the inside of the whole world.[18]

We will proceed from here with a look at the man himself. Chapter 1 offers a brief biographical sketch of Barfield that emphasizes his spiritual and intellectual development. Chapters 2 and 3 will explore the earliest and most important avenues through which Barfield's insights into the evolution of consciousness came: respectively, language and poetry. Chapters 3 and 4 will treat the evolution of consciousness more directly by exploring the idea

17. Barfield, *History, Guilt, and Habit*, 7. The designations of "inner" and "outer," which frequently occur in Barfield's writing, will be further explored and problematized in later chapters.

18. He continues: "Or, if we are using the term in its stricter sense—excluding therefore the subconscious mind—then it is a *part* of the inside of the whole world." Barfield, *History, Guilt, and Habit*, 11.

of "participation" in its original and final modes. We will then conclude by showing how Barfield's insights can shed light on what is often referred to as "the modern crisis of meaning."

1

Life

BORN IN LONDON DURING the final years of Queen Victoria's reign, Arthur Owen Barfield (1898–1997) was raised in a happy home with parents who were intent on cultivating his musical and literary sensibilities.[1] Mr. and Mrs. Barfield often played piano for their children and, as a family, they read aloud many classics of English literature. Though they did not disdain religion, little Owen's parents were decidedly agnostic. According to Simon Blaxland-de Lange, their home was one in which "a mood of scepticism reigned with regard to anything of a religious nature."[2] Though C. S. Lewis may have overstated the point, he wrote that Barfield was "brought up in a free-thinking family and so immune from all 'superstition' that he had hardly heard of Christianity itself until he went to school."[3]

In 1906, Barfield's parents sent him to Highgate School, where he received, in his own words, "the ordinary classical education that public schools provided in those days."[4] As G. B. Tennyson points out, however, from a more recent perspective, "this would have been a rich and challenging

---

1. The love for music that Barfield's parents instilled in him was so strong that Barfield later reflected, to the astonishment of those familiar with his work, that if he were forced to do without either music or poetry, he would do without poetry. See Zaleski and Zaleski, *Fellowship,* 99–100.

2. Blaxland-de Lange, *Owen Barfield,* 11.

3. Lewis went on to say that "the gospel first broke on Barfield in the form of a dictated list of Parables Peculiar to St. Matthew." *Surprised by Joy,* 206.

4. See Levin, dir., *Owen Barfield.*

curriculum, heavy in Latin and Greek grammar and literature, and now virtually unobtainable."[5] Fittingly, Highgate's chapel is where one of Barfield's greatest influences, the poet Samuel Taylor Coleridge, was buried.[6] Two important things took place during Barfield's time at Highgate. First, he formed what would prove to be a lifelong friendship with Cecil Harwood, who is important, among other reasons, because he and his wife would later introduce Barfield to the teachings of Rudolf Steiner. Second, Barfield developed a deep though inarticulate fascination with language, particularly poetic language, which would set the course of his entire career as a writer.

Many years later, Barfield recounted the moment at Highgate in which the power of poetic language first took hold of him.[7] He was sitting in a lesson on Latin grammar when the class was asked to translate the following sentence: "*Cato, octoginta annos natus, excessit e vita.*" The most obvious, though decidedly prosaic, rendering of this phrase in English is "Cato died at the age of eighty," but the boy sitting next to little Owen commented, with charming innocence, on the simple beauty of his own translation: "'Cato, at the age of eighty, *walked out of life*'—that's rather nice!" That boy was, of course, Cecil Harwood, and his remark gave Barfield pause. By that time, he was familiar with the concept of metaphor and had knowingly encountered figures of speech, but, in his words, he had not yet known "that it was possible to *enjoy* them, to relish them, for their own sake."[8] That moment, he said, marked the beginning of what would grow to be an intense love for language, and especially for *poetic* language. From the image of Cato, an old Roman statesman, "walking out of life," the most solemn mystery of mortal existence was irradiated with light; "death" took on a new life for the two boys, and Barfield took a small step toward his first great intellectual task.

Beginning in 1917, what may at first have seemed like a diversion from this task actually served to establish a foundation from which to proceed with it. During World War I, Barfield served two years in the Signals Service, a division of the Royal Engineers, but he never saw combat during his term of deployment. Instead, those years afforded him ample leisure to read widely and perfect the French that he had learned in school. Much of what he read during this time was English lyric poetry, especially from the so-called "Georgian poets" like Robert Graves, D. H. Lawrence, and Walter de la Mare (to Barfield's surprise and delight, de la Mare would, many years

---

5. Barfield, *Barfield Reader,* XV.

6. He was reburied at the neighboring St. Michael's parish church in 1965. Coleridge's grandson, Ernest Hartley Coleridge, was a Highgate pupil.

7. Barfield, "Owen Barfield and the Origin of Language."

8. Barfield, "Owen Barfield and the Origin of Language." (Barfield's emphasis.)

later, become a close friend and a devoted admirer of his work). The metaphors that Barfield encountered in poetry continued to reverberate in his consciousness as they had done in a rudimentary way during his years at Highgate. He reported having powerful experiences while reading poetry, especially lyric poems, that brought welcome relief to a growing sense of spiritual oppression that stemmed from his tacit acceptance of the scientific materialism of his age, which he had, by that point in his life, quite thoroughly absorbed.[9] The effects of his assumed materialism were exacerbated by the equally pervasive psychology of Freud: "[I] had imbibed from the whole of his 20th Century environment a suspicion, almost a conviction, that *any* theory implying that the world as a whole has any meaning, let alone a spiritual source, *must* be due to subjective wish-fulfillment." Barfield's experiences of transcendence through language would prove to be the primary impetus for his lifelong struggle to free himself and his readers from the paradigm of materialism, which, in his view, limited and conditioned the conceptions of so many otherwise sound thinkers, including those who had expressly rejected any kind of overtly materialist philosophy.[10] One of these galvanizing experiences—which he later referred to as his "sophia experience"—brought relief from a bout of depression that was, on the surface at least, occasioned by the pain of unrequited love. Upon reflection, however, Barfield concluded that he was not really in love with the young woman in question; he was simply enamored with the idea of love itself, and its promise to assuage the sense of meaninglessness that had been growing in his mind over the preceding years.[11] He later concluded that the root of his misery was in fact the conflict between his own inner life (which was being continually enriched by experiences he had while listening to music, dancing, and reading poetry) and his consciousness of the world around him, which, again, had been thoroughly inhibited by the straitjacket of materialistic thought: "Something inside me," he said, "seems to be so intensely and burningly alive, and everything around me so starkly dead."[12]

The so-called "sophia experience" came unexpectedly during a vacation to Switzerland. Unfortunately, Barfield's account of it is brief and sparingly

9. Barfield, "Owen Barfield and the Origin of Language."

10. One reason why Barfield esteemed Steiner so much (and why he was willing to rank Steiner's place in the history of thought with the likes of Aristotle) was that he believed that Steiner was the first, and possibly only, thinker in the history of modern Europe to fully disentangle himself with the paradigm of materialism. This is also why Barfield believed that anthroposophy held the key to the future health (indeed, survival) of the human race. See "Anthroposophy and the Future."

11. Blaxland-de Lange, *Owen Barfield*, 20.

12. Blaxland-de Lange, *Owen Barfield*, 20.

elaborated, though still interesting and suggestive. In his words, "the clouds sort of lifted," and "all the misery that I had felt, all this lifted with it."[13] Barfield said that this experience was important, not only because it restored a sense of meaning to his life, but also because "it is what led into the whole shape and development of my literary and philosophical work."[14] This is because Barfield would later find evidence, through his inquiries into the historical development of language and poetry, that such rare moments of elevated consciousness were not only more common but normal in ancient times. The contrast between the vitality of our inner experiences and our perception of an outer world that consists in inert and spiritually insignificant objects—a contrast of which Barfield himself had become so personally and painfully aware—was, in fact, distinctly modern. Contrary to being an objective fact about the world, this apparent antithesis was a decidedly subjective experience conditioned by a particular moment in history.

The opportunity and inclination to read widely during the war years ensured that Barfield was well prepared to enter Oxford's Wadham College after returning to England. There he read English literature and was awarded a first-class degree. He later earned a bachelor's of literature degree on the basis of a thesis that would eventually be revised and expanded into *Poetic Diction: A Study in Meaning* in 1928, a seminal work in the Barfield *corpus*.

It was in 1922, while working out his thesis, that Barfield and Harwood first encountered the writings of Rudolf Steiner. Initially, Barfield approached Steiner's work with decided skepticism. He soon found, however, to his surprise and delight that Steiner had not only corroborated many of the things he had been trying hard to articulate himself, but had also proceeded from them to build a comprehensive cosmology and philosophy of life, which he referred to as "anthroposophy." In the following years, Barfield continued to study Steiner's work, resulting in a transformation of his outlook which he described as follows: "first of all resistance, then gradual acceptance, with the one changing into the other by innumerable gradations of conviction, ending in a firm conviction that the findings of Rudolf Steiner's spiritual research are far and away our most reliable avenue in the direction of truth."[15] After overcoming his initial reluctance in respect to Steiner's abstruse and esoteric style (not improved by the haphazard translations that he was forced to rely upon before learning German), Barfield

13. Blaxland-de Lange, *Owen Barfield*, 20.

14. Barfield, *Poetic Diction*, 20.

15. Barfield, "Owen Barfield and the Origin of Language."

found that Steiner had already advanced many of the theories that he had been laboriously attempting to formulate for himself. He also found that Steiner had gone much further down what appeared to be the very same road that he was attempting to travel: "Steiner," he said, "had obviously forgotten volumes more than I had ever dreamed. . . . Some of my most daring and (as I thought) original conclusions were his premises."[16] In particular, Barfield observed, "Anthroposophy included and transcended not only my own poor stammering theory of poetry as knowledge, but the whole Romantic philosophy."[17] Barfield's growing conviction was further catalyzed by his realization that the changes in his own consciousness that he had experienced on occasion could be replicated and intensified as a result of the anthroposophical ideas and practices that gradually discipline and order one's imaginative faculties. Barfield and Harwood were so taken with Steiner's work that they both joined the Anthroposophical Society in 1923 and remained active members and passionate advocates of anthroposophy for the rest of their lives. Indeed, Barfield remained committed even after his baptism into the Anglican Church in 1949, maintaining (despite protests to the contrary from family and friends) that anthroposophy and Anglican theology are entirely compatible, if not complementary.

In the same year that Barfield first encountered Steiner, he also married Maud Douie, who shared with him, among other things, a passion for English folk dancing. Eventually, the couple moved to London, where Barfield attempted to make a living as a writer. During this time he contributed to various periodicals and produced several books, including *The Silver Trumpet*, *History in English Words,* and *Poetic Diction.* The significance of *The Silver Trumpet* is seen in that it is the first of the imaginative ventures into the fey realm, for which the Oxford Inklings later became famous.[18] After reading it for the first time, C. S. Lewis wrote in his diary that "nothing in its kind can be imagined better."[19] Much later, Lewis would lend his copy of *The Silver Trumpet* to J. R. R. Tolkien, who read it to his children. According to Lewis, the story was "the greatest success among his children that they have ever known." "In fine," Lewis concluded, "you have scored a direct hit."[20]

History in English Words and *Poetic Diction* are not only important because of their brilliant and highly original treatment of subjects ranging

16. Barfield, *Romanticism Comes of Age,* 12–13.

17. Barfield, *Romanticism Comes of Age,* 12–13.

18. Barfield's other fairy tales are less well-known, though deserving of more attention. "The Child and the Giant," for instance, is a fine specimen of the genre.

19. Lewis, *All My Roads,* 275.

20. Lewis, *Collected Letters of C. S. Lewis,* 198.

from history and language to poetry, but also because they are the twin pillars that support the entire edifice of Barfield's later work. Both implicitly contain—though approached from very different angles—the essential and recurrent theme of Barfield's writings, which he would spend the following decades laboring to make explicit: that is, his theory of the evolution of human consciousness. Indeed, this phrase "evolution of consciousness" already appears in a passage from *History in English Words*, and not only serves as a description of that particular project, but the task of elaborating it can be usefully understood as an *agendum* for Barfield's entire body of work.

> [I]n our own language alone, not to speak of its many companions, the past history of humanity is spread out in an imperishable map, just as the history of the mineral earth lies embedded in the layers of its outer crust. But there is a difference between the record of the rocks and the secrets which are hidden in language: whereas the former can only give us a knowledge of outward, dead things—such as forgotten seas and the bodily shapes of prehistoric animals and primitive men—language has preserved for us the inner, living history of man's soul. It reveals the evolution of consciousness.[21]

Poetic Diction further laid the foundation for Barfield's theory of the evolution of consciousness, and the book's memorable concluding passage makes it clear that Barfield was aware that this was the direction in which his future work was headed:

> Over the perpetual evolution of human consciousness, which is stamping itself upon the transformation of language, the spirit of poetry hovers, forever unable to alight. It is only when we are lifted above that transformation, so that we behold it as present movement, that our startled souls feel the little pat and the throbbing feathery warmth, which tell us that she has perched. It is only when we have risen from beholding the creature into beholding creation that our mortality catches for a moment the music of the turning spheres.[22]

In addition to the books discussed above, Barfield also worked on a novel during this time, called *English People*. Though *English People* is an interesting and well-crafted novel, it was never published. This is probably due to its length, its complexity, and the fact that it dealt with many themes that

---

21. Barfield, *History in English Words*, 14.
22. Barfield, *Poetic Diction*, 181.

did not, at that time, appeal to the fashions and interests of the English-speaking literati.[23]

Though the books that Barfield published in this period were received with enthusiasm by a number of distinguished readers, and continue to be enthusiastically studied today, none of them sold well enough to make Barfield's career as a writer sustainable. *History in English Words*, though not as widely read today, sold better than *Poetic Diction*. Barfield's own assessment was that the latter "was published at the worst possible moment for a book of that kind, just before the beginning of the 1930s, which saw a quite violent reaction in literary circles against anything in the nature of romanticism."[24] It was not long, then, until, in Barfield's words, he "virtually ceased pretending to be an author."[25] Growing financial concerns and mounting pressure from his father to join the family legal practice prompted him to abandon his ambitions toward a literary career and become a solicitor. The demands of his new occupation, along with the responsibilities that came with his and Maud's adoption of two children and fostering of another, made the next few decades of Barfield's life difficult. Remarkably, however, he was still able to publish many articles and reviews, mostly dealing with aspects of anthroposophy; these were later anthologized in a book called *Romanticism Comes of Age*. While it may seem as if anthroposophy provided relief from the tedium of his life as a London solicitor, it is clear that it was itself a source of distress as well as comfort. The distress came first from the tension it caused in his marriage. Maud, wishing that her husband would embrace a more conventionally Anglican faith, was uncomfortable with Barfield's involvement and was, at times, outright scornful of what she believed to be its heterodox teachings.[26] Additionally, the Anthroposophical Society was itself deeply divided among its members. As Blaxland-de Lange

23. Fortunately, the manuscript has been made available to the public on the Barfield Literary Estate website, though some chapters have gone missing. *The Rose on the Ash Heap*—which has been well described as "an apocalyptic fairy tale"—comes from the *English People* manuscript, and has been published independently.

24. It sold much better upon reissue in 1952 when there was, according to Barfield, "a sort of romantic reaction against anti-romanticism." From "Owen Barfield and the Origin of Language."

25. Barfield, "Owen Barfield and the Origin of Language."

26. Barfield's baptism into the Anglican Church was, no doubt, a result of genuine Christian desire and conviction, but it was also likely motivated by his desire to establish more common ground between himself and his wife, and also between himself and some of his friends (most notably C. S. Lewis). If this is correct, it seems that Maud appreciated it enough to return the favor. Barfield reported being quite moved when he found out that near the end of her life, Maud set aside her many reservations, had submitted an application for membership in the society of anthroposophists to which he belonged. See Blaxland-de Lange, *Owen Barfield*, 31.

notes, when Barfield reflected on his involvement in the society, his mind would continually return to the conflicts that broke out between various associations of anthroposophists, culminating in a total split in 1935.[27]

All this, combined with other personal troubles, including the death of his father, weighed heavily on Barfield's mind. So trying was this period of Barfield's career that he found himself, at one point, "on the verge of a nervous breakdown." Unsurprisingly, he tried (with evident success) to stave it off by writing a book: *This Ever Diverse Pair*. This humorous book, which turned out to sell relatively well, contains a fictional exploration of the tension between Barfield's true, natural, curious, and creative self ("Burgeon") with his false self ("Burden")—a mundane and tedious persona that he had developed in order to adapt to the pressures and demands of his life as a solicitor.[28]

As Barfield's legal career began drawing to a close, he was afforded more time for regular, uninterrupted study. He used this time efficiently, reading widely and keeping notes on many disparate subjects that interested him, ranging from language, philosophy and anthropology, to science (especially, he noted, unorthodox science).[29] Though the connections between these subjects and the unity behind the apparent multiplicity of thoughts that Barfield's notes recorded were obvious to him, he was unable, for a long time, to bring them all together into a single, coherent form. Inspiration finally arrived, however, by way of a book called *Aquinas and Kant: The Foundations of the Modern Sciences,* by Gavin Ardley, which discusses, among other things, the history and significance of the phrase "saving the appearances"—a phrase that has been attributed to Plato, and has played an important role in the development of natural philosophy and the modern science.[30] Through reflection on the meaning of this phrase, Barfield was afforded an insight into the fundamental unity that he had intuited but had been unable to apprehend directly behind the apparent diversity of ideas that he had been exploring over the preceding years. It was around this particular phrase, he said, that his accumulated mess of notes "seemed to

27. Blaxland-de Lange, *Owen Barfield*, 36.

28. It is worth noting that Jake Grefenstette offers a different interpretation, positing that these figures are embodiments of Imagination and Fancy, respectively. See Grefenstette, *"This Ever Diverse Pair* as an Apology for the Coleridgean Imagination."

29. Levin, dir., *Owen Barfield*.

30. In addition to *Saving the Appearances* itself, see C. S. Lewis's *Discarded Image*, 14–16. With specific reference to Barfield, Lewis provides a helpful summary of the significance that the notion expressed by this phrase has for understanding the causes and consequences of the Scientific Revolution.

crystallize in some way."[31] The result of this crystallization was a book appropriately titled *Saving the Appearances: A Study in Idolatry.*

In spite of its relative brevity, *Saving the Appearances* is the closest thing we have to a Barfieldian *summa.*[32] Whereas in prior books, Barfield's theory of the evolution of consciousness showed itself through the cracks, as it were, of his thought on other subjects (namely history, language, and poetry), in *Saving the Appearances* these subjects are reordered such that the evolution of consciousness serves as the sun around which they orbit. In this book, Barfield goads his readers into "a sustained acceptance, as distinct from mere theoretical admission, of the relation assumed by physical science to subsist between human consciousness on the one hand and, on the other, the familiar world of which that consciousness is aware."[33] Insofar as the reader persists in this, Barfield went on to show, standard accounts of natural and intellectual history are revealed to be deficient. This is largely because they do not take sufficient account of the role that consciousness plays in configuring what he refers to as the "familiar" or "phenomenal" world, and do not, therefore, account for the ways in which changes of consciousness have altered that configuration, causing fundamental transformations in the way that people perceive and relate to their surroundings (for Barfield, the phenomenal world is not, as the Cambridge Platonists insisted, a subjective illusion or "shadow show" that hides the real world, which consists entirely in formless quantities of matter; according to Barfield, the phenomenal world is, at least in a relevant sense, the "real" world).[34] Barfield goes on in *Saving the Appearances*, with a sweeping survey of the history of consciousness, to show how standard accounts of evolution would be different if they did not rely on the assumption that consciousness plays no role in configuring the phenomenal world, and how standard accounts of the history of ideas would be different if they accounted for the moving undercurrent of consciousness, which has conditioned not only what people have thought, but also the very act or process by which their thoughts have arisen.

In the latter part of the 1950s, after three decades of work in the legal profession, Barfield was able to fully retire. Growing interest in his work, especially in America, brought him many unexpected opportunities, including a number of visiting professorships and many invitations to speak to audiences about his own work, and, in the years following C. S. Lewis's death, about the life and writing of his closest friend. As Phillip and Carol Zaleski

---

31. Levin, dir., *Owen Barfield.*

32. Zaleski and Zaleski, *Fellowship,* 437.

33. Barfield, *Saving the Appearances,* 5.

34. Barfield, *History, Guilt, and Habit,* 11; 44–45.

note, growth of interest in Barfield's work notwithstanding, much of the fame that Barfield had achieved outside of certain academic circles stemmed from passages in Lewis's *Surprised by Joy* that laud Barfield's genius and explain the role that he played in Lewis's journey from atheism to Christianity.[35] Many of the invitations Barfield received, therefore, were to groups of Lewis's admirers. Much that Barfield said and wrote about his friend during this period has been collected and published under the title *Owen Barfield on C. S. Lewis*. Visiting professorships at numerous North American universities, however, were awarded on the basis of his own work, which had apparently caused a stir among certain faculties of English. Lectures that he gave at a few of these universities have been transcribed and published in *Speakers Meaning* and *History, Guilt, and Habit*. These short but illuminating books provide clear and succinct summaries of many important Barfieldian themes.

In addition to traveling and teaching, this period of Barfield's life brought him almost unprecedented freedom and leisure to write, which he did at an impressive pace. Along with the works already mentioned, he published a number of important books. *Worlds Apart*, for instance, depicts a fictional symposium that deals with much of the same content as *Saving the Appearances*. However, using the device of a symposium between specialists in different disciplines to great effect, Barfield was able to explore those ideas with more freedom and even audacity. T. S. Eliot, who was an admirer and sometime correspondent of Barfield, described the result well in saying that it is "[a] journey into seas of thought very far from ordinary routes of intellectual shipping."[36] Again in *Worlds Apart*, as in *Saving the Appearances*, Barfield attempts to show his reader that much of what he has argued about the evolution of human consciousness follows from a serious and sustained attempt to unify disparate bodies of knowledge that are, increasingly, kept in "water-tight compartments."[37] A few years later Barfield published *Unancestral Voice*, which is an esoteric and heavily anthroposophical novel. The years following were dedicated to the book in which Barfield would discharge his considerable intellectual debt to Samuel Taylor Coleridge: *What Coleridge Thought* (1971). With this magisterial study, entering as much into mainstream scholarship as he ever would, Barfield shows the intricate harmony behind what has appeared to many of Coleridge's readers as suggestive but discordant and underdeveloped thoughts. Though it won praise from many scholars, it was also criticized for presenting Coleridge's philosophy in a way

35. Zaleski and Zaleski, *Fellowship*, 480. This is also noted in R. J. Reilly's *Romantic Religion*, 13.

36. Barfield, *Worlds Apart*, back cover endorsement.

37. Owen Barfield, *Worlds Apart*, *passim*.

that sounds suspiciously similar to Barfield's own. Such criticisms are understandable since Barfield ascribes to Coleridge a rudimentary understanding of an evolution of consciousness that is distinct but not divisible from the evolution of nature and the history of ideas. At the same time, however, Barfield shows convincingly that Coleridge was truly his predecessor in the challenges he wished to present to the reigning scientific reality-principle. Several years later he published *The Rediscovery of Meaning*, a collection that includes some of Barfield's clearest and most profound essays.

Eventually, following his wife's death, Barfield settled back down in England. He wrote less, producing mainly short essays and a novella called *Eager Spring*, which links the wanton destruction of nature to the increasing tendency of people to think about the world in abstract terms, making "nature" appear spiritually insignificant; to appear, that is, as nothing more than a collection of material objects to be manipulated for human use. He welcomed correspondents and visitors who wished to discuss his own work as well as that of Lewis, Coleridge, and Steiner. One of his persistent concerns in the final years of his life, according to many of his visitors and correspondents, was the future of anthroposophy and the effect that he hoped it would have in renewing the intellectual, moral, and spiritual life of the human race. Barfield died at home on December 14, 1997, at the age of ninety-nine.

Since Barfield is most widely known for his membership in "the Oxford Inklings" and for his passionate advocacy of anthroposophy, both his role as an Inkling and as an anthroposophist will be briefly considered in the following sections. The remainder of the book will consider Barfield independently, as a profound and original thinker in his own right.

Barfield and the Inklings

Barfield is often remembered as one of the founding members of the famous group of Christian writers known as the Oxford Inklings. This remarkable circle of friends, which included such famous names as C. S. Lewis, J. R. R. Tolkien, and Charles Williams (among others), met frequently in the 1930s and forties for discussion and debate and provided each other with critical guidance on drafts of their writings, which they read aloud at meetings.

People often imagine that the Inklings was a much more formal association than it actually was. Warnie Lewis said that "[p]roperly speaking, the Inklings was neither a club nor a literary society, though it partook of the nature of both. . . . There were no rules, officers, agendas, or formal elections."[38] Many attempts have been made to say exactly what it is that bound this group together. While recognizing the many differences between its particular members, the Zaleskis characterize the general ethos of the group as follows: "their sympathies were mythological, medieval, and monarchical, and their great hope was to restore Western culture to its religious roots through Christian faith and pagan beauty."[39] Perhaps, with some of the lesser-known members in view (including, in some respects, Barfield himself), it is safer to accept the more general characterization provided by Lord David Cecil, who was himself a member: "The qualities . . . that gave The Inklings their distinctive personality were not primarily their opinions; rather it was a feeling for literature, which united, in an unusual way, scholarship and imagination."[40]

The Inklings usually met in Oxford pubs (especially The Eagle and Child aka "The Bird and Baby"), or in Lewis's quarters at Magdalen College. Since, for many years, Barfield lived away from Oxford with his family and maintained a demanding occupation as a solicitor, he was frequently unable to attend, and he did not know all of the members well. For this reason, some have questioned whether Barfield should be considered, as he often is, one of the group's central members, or whether he should be considered an important part of the group at all. These doubts about Barfield's importance to the Inklings are misguided, however. As Diana Glyer has argued, Lewis and his brother Warnie were certainly the group's social center, but there is at least a reasonable case to be made "for considering Owen Barfield as its true center, or at least its intellectual center."[41] This is because he was the earliest and (at times) the most profound exponent of many ideas and ideals that would later prove to define the group as a whole. In R. J. Reilly's words, "many of the romantic notions common to the members of the group exist in their most basic and radical form in his work."[42] It may be best, then, to describe Barfield not as central, but as *foundational* to the Inklings, or, more precisely, to the unintended theological and literary movement that, to this day, remains their living legacy.[43]

38. Quoted from Humphrey Carpenter's *Inklings*, 163. For a more recent survey and clarification, see King, "When Did the Inklings Meet?"

39. Zaleski and Zaleski, *Fellowship*, 5.

40. Zaleski and Zaleski, *Fellowship*, 198.

41. Gyler, "Centre of the Inklings." N.b.: Gyler does not ultimately conclude that Barfield was the center of the Inklings. Her contention is that "center" is the wrong way to think about the relation of any one Inkling to the others. Nevertheless, her point stands: Barfield's contribution to the intellectual character of the group was essential.

42. Reilly, *Romantic Religion*, 12. This passage is also quoted by Gyler in "Centre of the Inklings."

43. Due to his long life, Barfield has often been called "the first and last Inkling."

Barfield and C. S. Lewis

Barfield and C. S. Lewis met in 1919 as students at Oxford University. They were drawn together by mutual recognition of each other's genius. But it was immediately obvious that they agreed on very little. For this reason, Lewis famously characterized Barfield as his "Second Friend."[44] In contrast to the "First Friend," who Lewis described as an *alter ego,*" the Second Friend is "the anti-self."[45] The First agrees with you on everything, and shares what you consider to be your most idiosyncratic beliefs, desires, and delights. The Second, in contrast, is a person with whom you agree on little. Again, elaborating on the type of the Second Friend, with particular reference to Barfield, Lewis wrote: "Of course he shares your interests; otherwise he would not become your friend at all. But he has approached them all at a different angle. He has read all the right books but has got the wrong thing out of every one." And later: "When you set out to correct his heresies, you find that he forsooth has decided to correct yours! And then you go at it, hammer and tongs, far into the night, night after night, or walking through fine country that neither gives a glance to, each learning the weight of the other's punches, and often more like mutually respectful enemies than friends."[46] Lewis makes it clear that his intense and incessant disputes with Barfield were not a barrier to the formation of a deep and lasting bond; on the contrary, for two vigorous young men with such extraordinary intellectual gifts, the *joie de guerre* was an ideal catalyst of friendship.

In those days, Lewis was an atheist, and he regarded any and all claims about the supernatural to be nonsensical. He was therefore "hideously shocked" when he found out that Barfield and their mutual friend Harwood

---

This is not strictly true, of course. Both Williams and Tolkien were born before him and some other lesser-known members outlived him. Nevertheless it is an apt description in another sense. Barfield was a founding member of the group and his stature was such that, to borrow words from the Zaleskis, "when Barfield closed his eyes, the life of the great Inklings came to an end." *Fellowship,* 505.

44. Lewis, *Surprised by Joy,* 199.

45. Lewis, *Surprised by Joy,* 199. Barfield's "First friend" was Cecil Harwood, who was also friends with Lewis. Barfield, Harwood, and Lewis were close for the entirety of their adult lives and took frequent walking tours together, which are wonderfully described, among other places, in Laurence Harwood's *C. S. Lewis, My Godfather.*

46. Lewis continued: "Actually (though it never seems so at the time) you modify one another's thought; out of this perpetual dog-fight a community of mind and a deep affection emerge. But I think he changed me a good deal more than I him. Much of the thought which he afterwards put into *Poetic Diction* had already become mine before that important little book appeared. It would be strange if it had not. He was of course not so learned then as he has since become; but the genius was already there." Lewis, *Surprised by Joy,* 199–200.

had embraced the teachings of Rudolf Steiner and become anthroposo-phists.[47] As a result of Barfield's "conversion," he and Lewis's usual arguments intensified. Indeed, they entered into a period that Lewis jokingly referred to as the "Great War" between himself and Barfield. This was a years-long dispute that took place both in each other's homes, on long walking tours through the English countryside, and by correspondence. Though Lewis went to great lengths to rebuff Barfield's arguments, he found, in the end, that he was greatly affected by them. Indeed, many years after their Great War subsided, Lewis said that it was one of the major turning points of his life.

For a number of reasons, it is difficult to say exactly what the Great War was about. Lewis made it clear that its occasion was Barfield's acceptance of anthroposophy, but the specific matters of dispute appear to have been an eclectic cluster of Barfield's newly formed beliefs about the nature and function of the imagination. If a crux is to be identified, it would be the role that the imagination plays in both perception and knowledge. Barfield (fol-lowing Steiner) believed that the imagination has an indispensable role to play in both the determination and discernment of truth. Lewis disagreed, as is evident from words that he would later write: the imagination, he said, is "the organ of meaning . . . which is the antecedent condition both of truth and falsehood, whose antithesis is not error but nonsense." Reason, on the other hand, Lewis described as "the natural organ of truth."[48] For Barfield, the search for truth was at least partially an affair of the imagination, but for Lewis it was wholly rational.[49] Though Lewis had abandoned materialism, Barfield believed that he had failed to grasp "the epistemological signifi-cance of the imagination" because he had failed to fully disentangle himself from "the paradigm of materialism."[50] In other words, he had ceased to profess an explicit belief in materialism but tacitly persisted in situat-ing his views within a materialistic matrix. Noteworthy, however, is the sympathy that Lewis had for Barfield's position—a sympathy that was not

47. Lewis, *Surprised by Joy*, 206.

48. Lewis, "Bluspels and Flalansferes," in *Selected Literary Essays*, 265.

49. Barfield later said: "That's what the Great War was about, whether imagination is a vehicle of truth or whether it is simply a highly desirable and pleasurable experi-ence of the human soul." He went on to say that Lewis's preference for the latter answer "is partly [what] prevented his getting any happy relationship with anthroposophy." *Owen Barfield on C. S. Lewis*, 143. See Lionel Adey's *C. S. Lewis' 'Great War' with Owen Barfield* and Stephen Thorson's *Joy and Poetic Imagination* for in-depth treatments of Lewis and Barfield's argument.

50. Barfield believed, however, that Lewis did start to break free of the paradigm in his later years. He was able to do so, Barfield thought, by grasping "the notion of imagi-nation as a vehicle of knowledge as well as feeling through his idea of the Sacrament." *Owen Barfield on C. S. Lewis*, 29.

reciprocated. This is evident, for example, in the concession that follows Lewis's pronouncement about the imagination and reason just quoted:

> It is, I confess, undeniable that such a view indirectly implies a kind of truth or rightness in the imagination itself. . . . And thence, I confess, it does follow that if our thinking is ever true, then the metaphors by which we think must have been good metaphors. It does follow that if those original equations, between good and light, or evil and dark, between breath and soul and all the others, were from the beginning arbitrary and fanciful—if there is not, in fact, a kind of psycho-physical parallelism (or more) in the universe—then all our thinking is nonsensical. But we cannot, without contradiction, believe it to be nonsensical.[51]

The full significance of these words will, we hope, become clearer in the following chapters.

Though Barfield and Lewis never reached full agreement, they forced one another to flesh out their respective positions with greater nuance and clarity, and to refine the arguments they used in support of them. Lewis, more than Barfield, was changed by the dispute. In *Surprised by Joy,* he recalled two important effects that the Great War had on him, both of which are important because (though he didn't realize it at the time) they broke down his intellectual defenses against theism and prepared the way for his eventual acceptance of Christianity.

The first effect, Lewis said, was that "[Barfield] made short work of what I have called my 'chronological snobbery.'"[52] By this he meant "the uncritical acceptance of the intellectual climate common to our own age and the assumption that whatever has gone out of date is on that account discredited."[53] Secondly, Barfield forced him to concede that the staunch epistemological realism that they had both formerly accepted was incompatible with other commitments they shared about the validity and reliability of reason, and about the nature of consciousness and its relation to the material world. Additionally, Barfield convinced Lewis that his epistemological commitments were incompatible with materialism, which entails a stringent skepticism that Lewis was unwilling to accept. For the sake of consistency, then, Lewis had to give up his materialism and admit that "mind was no late-come epiphenomenon; that the whole universe was, in the last resort, mental; that our logic was participation in a cosmic *Logos.*"[54] This admission would later

51. Lewis, "Bluspels and Flalansferes," in *Selected Literary Essays,* 265.
52. Lewis, *Surprised by Joy,* 207.
53. Lewis, *Surprised by Joy.*
54. Lewis, *Surprised by Joy,* 209. The idea of logic as a "participation in a cosmic

be used as a crucial premise in the argument for theism that Lewis made in his book *Miracles: A Preliminary Study.*

Barfield and Lewis remained close friends and interlocutors until Lewis's death in 1963. Of the many moving tributes that they made to each other over the years, none more concisely captures not only their affection, but also their mutual intellectual and imaginative debts, than the acknowledgments and dedications they made to each other respectively in *Poetic Diction* and *The Allegory of Love.* In 1951, in the preface to the second edition of *Poetic Diction,* Barfield said that he dedicated the book to Lewis, not in an attempt to claim any credit for the considerable distinction that Lewis had gained since its original publication, but, rather, "in celebration of nearly a lifetime's priceless friendship."[55] The dedication includes a well-selected line from William Blake's *Marriage of Heaven and Hell:* "To C. S. Lewis, 'opposition is true friendship.'" After thanking many of his friends and colleagues, Lewis concluded his own acknowledgments in *The Allegory of Love* as follows: "Above all, the friend to whom I have dedicated this book has taught me not to patronize the past, and has trained me to see the present itself as a 'period.' I desire for myself no higher function than to be one of the instruments whereby his theory and practice in such matters may become more widely effective."[56] The dedication reads "To Owen Barfield, wisest and best of my unofficial teachers."

Barfield and J. R. R. Tolkien

Barfield and J. R. R. Tolkien met, as most of the Inklings did, as mutual friends of C. S. Lewis. Barfield provided an amusing account of the night they were introduced: "How many evenings out of the many hundreds, or rather thousands, that have sunk without trace, can I easily remember whenever I want to?" he asked. And his answer was "[v]ery few indeed."

---

logos" is an old one, but Barfield's case was built primarily on the expression of it that he found in Steiner: "Paradoxical as it may sound, it is the truth: the Idea which Plato conceived and the like idea which I conceive are not two ideas. It is one and the same idea. And there are not two ideas: one in Plato's head and one in mine; but in the higher sense Plato's head and mine interpenetrate each other; all heads interpenetrate which grasp one and the same idea; and this idea is only once there as a single idea. It is there; and the heads all go to one and the same place in order to have this idea in them." Rudolf Steiner, *Mystics of the Renaissance and Their Relation to Modern Thought,* 37.

55. Barfield, *Poetic Diction,* 38.

56. Lewis, *Allegory of Love,* x. Barfield was profoundly grateful for these words, but also puzzled by them. For more, see "C. S. Lewis and Historicism" anthologized in *Owen Barfield on C. S. Lewis.*

One of the few that Barfield did profess to remember clearly, however, was an evening in the 1920s when Lewis introduced Barfield to Tolkien. He went on to describe that evening as follows:

> We dined together at the Eastgate Hotel, nearly opposite Magdalen College, Oxford. In those days there was as yet no *Hobbit*, no *Lord of the Rings*, no *Screwtape*, no Inklings even. For some reason Tolkien was in a ridiculously combative mood and seemed to me to contradict nearly everything I said—or more often what he (wrongly) assumed I was just going to say—before I had even got as far as saying it. But although Lewis actually apologised for him when we were alone afterwards, there was no occasion for it. The whole conversation was so entirely good-humoured and enjoyable . . . I have never had a conversation quite like it before or since.[57]

Tolkien and Barfield continued to see each other from time to time at Inklings meetings over the coming years, and they took at least two long walking tours together with Lewis, but these meetings were infrequent and Barfield later said that, because of the conditions under which their meetings took place, he never got to speak with Tolkien at length or in depth. That is why later in life, Barfield said with regret that he did not know Tolkien well, though the time they spent together left a lasting impression on him. Tolkien seems to have appreciated Barfield's presence in Inklings meetings, not least because of his unique ability to keep Lewis in check. In a letter to his son, in which he described a meeting of the Inklings, Tolkien wrote that "O. B. is the only man who can tackle C. S. L. making him define everything and interrupting his most dogmatic pronouncements with subtle distinguo's."[58]

Despite the fact that Barfield and Tolkien did not know each other well, careful readings of both men's work reveal some deep affinities between them, and at least some of those affinities can be attributed to the influence that Barfield's early writings, especially *Poetic Diction*, had on Tolkien.[59] This is particularly conspicuous in the development of Tolkien's Middle-earth legendarium that arose in connection to his invented languages, for, in Tolkien's words, "a language requires a suitable habitation, and a history in

57. Barfield, "Foreword."

58. Tolkien continued: "The result was a most amusing and highly contentious evening on which (had an outsider eavesdropped) he would have thought it a meeting of fell enemies hurling deadly insults before drawing their guns." *Letters of J. R. R. Tolkien*, 103.

59. For the most in-depth treatment of connections between Barfield and Tolkien's thought, see the revised edition of Verlyn Flieger's *Splintered Light*.

which it can develop."[60] This is important because it is Tolkien's understanding of the history of language that was distinctively Barfieldian. According
to Lewis, Tolkien once stated that Barfield's "theory of ancient semantic
unity" (i.e., the theory about the development of language explored in chapter 2) "had modified his whole outlook, and he was always just going to
say something in a lecture when your concept stopped him in time." Lewis
continued by saying that "It is one of those things that when you've seen it
there are all sorts of things you can never say again."[61] Recognizing Tolkien's
claim that his writings on Middle-earth sprung from an attempt to invent
languages that were historically rooted, Verilyn Flieger states that "The languages of Middle-earth in their development are so striking an illustration
of Barfield's thesis that one might almost think Tolkien had kept *Poetic Diction* open before him as he worked."[62]

Tolkien even alludes to Barfield's theory of ancient semantic unity in a
brief but very suggestive remark in *The Hobbit*. Those who understand this
theory, and the wider implications it has for how the character of ancient
forms of consciousness should be conceived, will appreciate the significance
of the allusion, which is found in chapter 12: "To say that Bilbo's breath was
taken away is no description at all. There are no words left to express his
staggerment, since Men changed the language that they learned of elves in
the days when all the world was wonderful." Commenting on this passage
in a letter to his publisher, Tolkien notes the connection to Barfield: "The
only philological remark (I think) in *The Hobbit* is . . . an odd mythological
way of referring to linguistic philosophy, and a point that will (happily) be
missed by any who have not read Barfield."

Many other interesting and fruitful connections can be made between
Tolkien and Barfield. For instance, as Humphrey Carpenter pointed out,
there are clear echoes of Barfield in Tolkien's critique of Max Müller's view
of myth as "a disease of language."[63] According to Müller, the ancient myths
came about when, in order to express new, abstract notions about the origin
and function of nature, primitive people used metaphors that were mistaken
by later generations as literal descriptions. Barfield, by that point, had for
many years been engaging and criticizing Müller's work with particular and
repeated emphasis on the fallacy inherent in this view. Though he does not

60. *Letters of J. R. R. Tolkien*, 374–375.

61. Quoted from Carpenter, *Inklings*, 42.

62. Flieger, *Splintered Light*, 68. Similarly, it has several times been observed that
Tolkien's poem "Mythopoeia" can be fruitfully read as a concise poetic expression of
one of the primary theses that Barfield labored to establish in *Poetic Diction*.

63. Carpenter, *Inklings*, 121–22.

mention Barfield, Tolkien later succinctly summarized the kind of position that Barfield had ascertained as the true alternative to Müller's conclusions:

> Max Müller's view of mythology as a "disease of language" can be abandoned without regret. Mythology is not a disease, though it may like all human things become diseased. You may as well say that thinking is a disease of the mind. It would be more near the truth to say that languages, especially modern European languages, are a disease of mythology. But language cannot, all the same, be dismissed. The incarnate mind, the tongue, and the tale are in our world coeval.[64]

Barfield the Anthroposophist

Since a number of references have been made to anthroposophy, and since anthroposophy was of immense importance to Barfield's own intellectual and spiritual development, we will briefly explore some of its distinctive elements. This is not an easy task, however. As many of its adherents readily admit, the essence of anthroposophy is elusive, and resists precise formulation. In a certain way, the difficulty is very similar to that which presented itself in our attempt to define the Inklings. Though anthroposophy has many religious implications, it is not itself a religion and has adherents from many faiths. It can most accurately, albeit vaguely, be described as the philosophy of Rudolf Steiner, and anthroposophists can be understood as active adherents of Steiner's philosophy. We can look to Steiner himself for a more elaborate definition of the term, which he offered in a lecture delivered in Stuttgart, February 13, 1923:

> The term "Anthroposophy" should really be understood as synonymous with "Sophia," meaning the content of consciousness, the soul attitude and experience that make a man a full-fledged human being. The right interpretation of "Anthroposophy" is not "the wisdom of man," but rather "the consciousness of one's humanity." In other words, the reversing of the will, the

64. There is little to say about the connection between Barfield and the other widely known Inkling, Charles Williams. Barfield once reflected that he may have discovered much in common between himself and Williams if he had had adequate time to speak to him outside of the Inklings meetings, which were, by all accounts, not conducive to one-on-one conversation. Williams once wrote a positive, though quite selective review of Barfield's *Romanticism Comes of Age,* and Barfield admits deep admiration of Williams's theology while also criticizing it for inadequately addressing concerns about the effects of the incarnation on those who lived before it. *Saving the Appearances,* 169. For more, see Dunning, "Charles Williams and Owen Barfield."

experiencing of knowledge, and one's participation in the time's destiny, should all aim at giving the soul a certain direction of consciousness, a "Sophia."[65]

Hence, it can be seen that the essence of anthroposophy is to be understood more as a consciously cultivated disposition than a set system of doctrines (a distinction which is, regrettably, all too often lost on some of Steiner's more ardent disciples). Nevertheless, despite the fact that no well-defined system of doctrines form the essence of anthroposophy, anthroposophists have, for the most part, been united in acceptance of some distinctive aspects of Steiner's worldview.

This worldview began to take shape in the latter part of the nineteenth century, when Steiner was invited to be the editor of a new edition of Goethe's writings on the natural sciences. Inspired by Goethe's holistic method of proto-phenomenological scientific research, Steiner began to reenvision the nature and limits of science for himself. Steiner's departure point in his anthroposophical teachings can perhaps be understood as an application of Goethe's scientific method to human consciousness itself. The external fruition of Steiner's approach appeared as his first and greatest major work, the title of which is usually translated as *The Philosophy of Freedom* but which is perhaps more accurately denoted by its subtitle: *Results of Introspective Observation According to the Method of Natural Science*. Steiner himself, sensing the misleading associations that the main title would evoke for many of his English-speaking readers, preferred it to be known in English as "The Philosophy of Spiritual Activity." In this book, he attempted to lead the reader to the point of immediate observation of his or her own process of cognition. Steiner insisted that all of his later thought, which was to flower in the development of anthroposophy and all of its practical offshoots, was contained in *The Philosophy of Freedom* in the way that a seed contains all of the future manifestations of the plant in a state of potency.

For a time Steiner occupied an influential position in the Theosophical movement. Though he was something of an informal leader among theosophists in Germany, he never became an official member of the society, and maintained a number of reservations about its teaching. His disagreements with the Theosophical Society culminated in his refusal to recognize a young Indian boy—Jiddu Krishnamurti—as the reincarnation of Jesus Christ, in spite of the Society's insistence on the truth of this identification.[66] The result of Steiner's rejection of the society's assertion

65. Steiner, "Awakening to Community."

66. After some time had passed, that pupil, Jiddu Krishnamurti, also rejected this claim.

led to an irreparable falling out with Annie Besant (then president of the society). Scandalized by the claim that Krishnamurti was a reincarnation of Christ, Steiner, along with many German theosophists, broke away from the Theosophical Society ultimately to form, under Steiner's leadership, the new Anthroposophical Society. Among many ways in which the Anthroposophical Society differed from its predecessor was its positive emphasis on the intellectual and spiritual inheritance of the West.[67] Additionally, Anthroposophy differs from Theosophy in the willingness that Steiner and many other anthroposophists have shown to engage philosophy, science, and other fields of inquiry with respect and rigor. On the other hand, as R. J. Reilly has pointed out, "Theosophy is hardly philosophical at all, but it is rather a mystery religion, a modern Gnosticism . . . it is 'occult' in the usual modern sense of that term."[68] Perhaps most fundamentally, Anthroposophy departed from Theosophy in its emphasis on the centrality of Christ in its interpretation of history and human evolution. Barfield neatly summed up the Anthroposophical view in his 1957 work *Saving the Appearances:*

> I believe that the blind-spot which posterity will find most startling in the last hundred years or so of Western civilization is, that it had, on the one hand, a religion which differed from all others in its acceptance of time, and of a particular point in time, as a cardinal element in its faith: that it had, on the other hand, a picture in its mind of the history of the earth and man as an evolutionary process; and that it neither saw nor supposed any connection whatever between the two.[69]

Of course, the Anthroposophical Society was much more than an association of esoteric philosophers. Members quickly began embarking on practical initiatives to apply Steiner's teachings in literature, art, education, medicine, and agriculture. Many anthroposophists have been active in promoting social reforms in line with Steiner's idea of a threefold social order in which the cultural, political, and economic spheres are sufficiently separated that each is able to make its proper and autonomous contribution

---

67. Steiner was nonetheless steeped in spiritual and intellectual traditions of the East, and many of their distinctive elements are central to his thought. As R. J. Reilly noted, "Anthroposophy does not ignore Eastern thought . . . but it attempts to systematize it. The Buddhist doctrine of maya—of the phenomenal world as illusion, or of matter itself as unreal—contains an element of truth for the Anthroposophist, as it did for romantics like Emerson and Coleridge and Goethe, who often described the phenomenal world as spiritual in essence but perceived under the mode of matter." Reilly, *Romantic Religion,* 16.

68. Reilly, *Romantic Religion,* 16.

69. Barfield, *Saving the Appearances,* 167.

to the whole of society. The threefold vision of society, according to Steiner, fosters the conditions under which principles of justice and democracy can be best upheld and economic prosperity can be achieved without undermining the flourishing of a robust cultural life by demanding that works of science, art, religion, and philosophy be compelled to justify themselves before the political authorities or according to their economic payoff.[70]

One of the more distinctive features of Steiner's thought, as suggested by the subtitle of *The Philosophy of Freedom*, is his belief in the possibility of objective spiritual research. While almost everyone accepts the possibility of objective research of the physical world by way of our senses and the scientific method, Steiner argued that it was no less possible to undertake objective research from departure points among the non-sensory elements of our experience, which may be neatly summed up under the rubric of thinking, feeling, and willing. Because this is a book about Barfield's thought and not about Steiner's teachings *per se* (except so far as they are reflected in the former), this brief introduction to anthroposophy will have to suffice. That being said, Barfield shared many elements of Steiner's vision and hence we will have occasion to return to Steiner later in the present work.

70. Many who, unlike Barfield, are uninterested or even suspicious of the more esoteric aspects of Steiner's thought have nevertheless been attracted to him as a prognosticator of modern spiritual decline, and have found much to admire in his practical suggestions toward spiritual renewal. One famous example is Albert Schweitzer, who wrote the following words after meeting him for the first time: "One of us, I no longer remember which one, began to speak of the spiritual decline of culture as the fundamental, unremarked problem of our times. We realized that both of us were occupied with this question; neither had expected this of the other. . . . Each of us experienced from one another that we had taken on the same mission in life: to strive for the rise of true culture enlivened and formed by humane ideals, and to stimulate people to become truly thoughtful human beings. We took leave of one another in this consciousness of solidarity. . . . We each followed one another's work. To take part in Rudolf Steiner's high flight of thought of spiritual science was not given to me. I know, however, that in this he lifted up and renewed many people, and his disciples attained exceptional accomplishments in many realms. I have rejoiced at the achievement which his great personality and his profound humanity have brought about in the world." Schweitzer, *Werke aus dem Nachlaß*, 229–31.

2

Language

MOST THINKERS IN THE history of the West have assumed (and sometimes forcibly asserted) that words are best understood simply as labels. Consensus among speakers, it is believed, affixes these labels to discrete and static things, both tangible and intangible. As a result, the differences between languages (even languages far removed in place and time) have often been viewed, to borrow words from David Bentley Hart, as nothing more than "distinct ways of expressing identical meanings (which apparently float above the flux of language and culture like Platonic ideas)."[1] This broad consensus began to fray in the eighteenth century when, according to Barfield, "a more historical conception of philology began to spread rapidly over Europe."[2] During this period, interest in a historical approach to the study of language was greatly stimulated by the development of methods by which speculations about the history of words could be evaluated. Using these methods, scholars were able to amass, at an unprecedented speed, vast amounts of reliable information on the historical development of individual words. As a result, patterns of development in language as a whole became, for the first time, easily discernible. This new perspective on language caused many scholars to discard the commonly assumed view of words as labels affixed to discrete and timeless objects or ideas and adopt, instead, a more historical and developmental view of words and their meanings. Barfield himself

1. Hart, "Reply to N. T. Wright."
2. Barfield, *Poetic Diction*, 60.

31

eloquently captured the spirit of this view when he described the meanings of words as "flashing, iridescent shapes like flames—ever-flickering vestiges of the slowly evolving consciousness beneath them."[3] To use the jargon of contemporary linguistics, the emphasis shifted from a synchronic approach to language, such as that assumed (at least provisionally) by the grammarian, to a diachronic or genealogical approach. This transition gave birth to the modern forms of several distinct but related fields of inquiry including philology, etymology, and historical linguistics.

It is worth noting that this change in the manner by which language is understood and studied was not an isolated phenomenon. At that time, historical consciousness was on the rise in many disciplines besides philology, especially the sciences. Physicists were learning that time was a dimension that was ineluctable from any coherent consideration of the material world. No longer was the universe imagined to have existed since the beginning in more or less its present configuration. Instead, new theories and discoveries were leading to an increasingly dynamic and evolutionary view of cosmic history. Barfield noted a similar trend among biologists when he observed that they were abandoning their formerly prominent belief that "the variety of natural species and the secrets of their relation to each other can be understood apart from their history."[4] Nevertheless, whereas Darwinism seemed to take the world by storm, acceptance of the fact that linguistics, no less than biology, must be understood in terms of its history was a much more dilatory process. Indeed, even today, the historical view of language has scarcely penetrated the consciousness of the average person as deeply or thoroughly as Darwin's theory of biological evolution had already done by the beginning of the twentieth century. Neither has it fully taken root among the *intelligentsia*. Like pre-Darwinian biologists, Barfield lamented that many thinkers "still seek to confine the science of language, as the Linnaeans once confined botany, within a sort of network of timeless abstractions."[5]

As the historical study of language developed in depth and sophistication, discoveries were made that not only corroborated the isolated transformations of verbal forms and meanings that were already known but also seemed to suggest identifiable trends that have played themselves out through history; the development of language as such appeared to be evolutionary. Barfield noted one interesting example of this in an essay entitled "Philology and the Incarnation." In it, he identified a large class of English

3. Barfield, *Poetic Diction*, 75.
4. Barfield, *Saving the Appearances*, 116.
5. Barfield, *Saving the Appearances*.

words that describe qualities of things in the outside world in reference to the effect they have on an observer, rather than simply describing the things themselves. Examples include words like *charming, enchanting, depressing*, and so on. Grammatically, all these are present participles of verbs in the active voice, which in itself does not present any difficulty to the conventional theories of the genesis of language. But philologists had succeeded in demonstrating that this class of words suddenly and inexplicably shifted their application during a particular period in the history of the English language. Barfield used the word *charming* to illustrate this phenomenon: "Grammatically . . . when we speak of an object, a garden, for instance, or a landscape, or perhaps a person, as charming, we make that object or person the subject of a verb which denotes activity of some sort. That is what we do grammatically, but it is not at all, or only very rarely, what we mean semantically."[6] What *is* meant semantically is best seen by considering the example of a charming child. Rarely, by this description, does a person mean to indicate what a strict and pedantic grammarian may be inclined to say that it *technically* indicates, which is that the child is actively attempting to charm those around it. Indeed, Barfield points out, "the charmer who is charming in the verbal sense generally ceases to be charming in the adjectival sense!"[7]

This discrepancy between grammar and semantics is curious enough, but even more curious is the fact that it is not obviously present in English prior to the sixteenth century. What can account for the sudden rise of this linguistic phenomenon wherein things in the outer world begin to be described almost exclusively in reference to the effect they have on the inner world of the observer? "Is the appearance of these words at this comparatively late state just something that happened to happen," Barfield asked, "or is it a surface manifestation of deeper currents of some sort?"[8] Unsurprisingly, Barfield opted for the latter explanation, for experience had taught him the immense significance of such observations. "It is impossible," he wrote,

> to give much attention to words and their meanings, and more especially the history of words and the history of the changes which those meanings have undergone, without making a number of interesting discoveries. Moreover, in my experience the discoveries one then makes are of a kind which it is impossible

6. Barfield, "Philology and the Incarnation," in *Rediscovery of Meaning and Other Essays*, 338–339.

7. Barfield, "Philology and the Incarnation," in *Rediscovery of Meaning and Other Essays*.

8. Barfield, "Philology and the Incarnation," in *Rediscovery of Meaning and Other Essays*, 340.

to make without being forced by them to reflect rather inten-
sively on the whole nature of man and of the world in which he
lives.[9]

As we shall see, Barfield believed that these sudden changes in the use of
language are best explained in terms of corresponding changes in human
consciousness. This particular change, though, is but one wave in the turning tide; a notable event but only one of many in a larger trend of development in meaning over time. "One swallow doth not a summer make," as
Aesop may have put it.

Perhaps the best way to characterize the trajectory of this larger trend
is to say that it consisted in a transformation of language from concreteness to abstraction. Words with particular, material, and tangible references
that characterize primitive forms of language appeared to have given way to
the largely abstract and intangible meanings that populate the vocabular-
ies of many modern languages. That much had been inferred from basic
philological inquiry, and Barfield was familiar with this consensus. Thus,
in *Poetic Diction* he observed: "If we trace the meanings of a great many
words—or those of the elements of which they are composed—about as far
back as etymology can take us, we are at once made to realize that an over-
whelming proportion, if not all, of them referred in earlier days to one of
these two things—a solid sensible object, or some animal (probably human)
activity."[10] Barfield returned to the same point in *Saving the Appearances,*
and offers several examples:

> It is a commonplace of [etymology] that, whatever word we hit
> on, if we trace its meaning far enough back, we find it apparently
> expressive of some tangible, or at all events, perceptible object
> or some physical activity. *Understanding* once meant "standing
> under," and abstractions like *concept* and *hypothesis* merely dis-
> guise, in the garb of a dead language, a similarly humble origin.
> Even *right* and *wrong* are said to have once meant "straight" and
> "sour."[11]

Of course, if Barfield's work had only reiterated what was already "a commonplace" of etymology at the time, there would likely be little reason to
return to it today. Indeed, to illuminate the significance that Barfield found
in this fact is precisely the purpose of this book—and if anything less than

9. Barfield, "Philology and the Incarnation," in *Rediscovery of Meaning and Other
Essays,* 338.

10. Barfield, *Poetic Diction,* 63–64.

11. Barfield, *Saving the Appearances,* 116.

a book were necessary to accomplish this, then no book would likely be necessary to begin with, as this knowledge would already have become, by itself, a commonplace.

Returning to the state of philology in Barfield's time: that languages tended to develop according to the trend outlined above was widely known is not to say that it was of no interest. On the contrary, it was a subject of extensive speculation not only among philologists, but among many eminent philosophers as well. The latter, like Barfield, sought to understand how the historical development of language could fit into the larger context of the history of ideas and anthropological theories of human evolution. Put another way, these thinkers wished to achieve a theory adequate to understand why this change in language transpired in just the way that it did. Thinkers as far back as John Locke had already tried their hand at theorizing over this issue. Though the science of etymology was only in its infancy in his time, Locke had access to sufficient historical records to correctly conjecture what etymologists would later confirm. To Locke, that the transformation of language from concreteness to abstraction served as support for his foregone theory of knowledge through empiricism: "I doubt not," he said," but, if we could trace [all words] to their sources, we should find, in all languages, the names which stand for things that fall not under our senses to have had their first rise from sensible ideas."[12] Though Locke's enunciation may at first glance appear to be a scarcely disguised recapitulation of the so-called "Peripatetic axiom" of the scholastic philosophers—*nihil est in intellectu quod non sit prius in sensu*[13]—Locke actually marshaled this proposition in opposition to the realism of Aristotle and many of the medieval schoolmen. By "the names which stand for things," Locke means roughly "the labels which stand for discrete objects whose external similarity leads us to designate them with a common term." In other words, the names of things are merely *nominal*, which is to say, a product of convention and nothing more. For the scholastic *realists*, by contrast, the reason that we designate similar objects with a common term is that they are, in reality, similar. This is to say that they share not only in appearance or in material composition, but in reality: hence, "realism." "Nothing is in the intellect that was not first in the senses" because it is by way of the senses that we are able to apprehend the reality of things. Locke, however, sounding the fruition of nominalism and the keynote of modern empiricism, asserted that names are derived from knowledge won through sensory experience alone because reality is limited

12. Locke, *Essay Concerning Human Understanding*, Bk. III, Ch. 2.

13. "Nothing is in the intellect that was not first in the senses"; Cf. Thomas Aquinas, *De veritate*, q. 2 a. 3 arg. 19.

to what is perceptible to the senses and hence, sensory knowledge is the only kind of knowledge that there is.

Locke has proved to be a seminal figure in the development of modern scientific epistemology, and in the demoting of philosophy from "Queen of the Sciences" to their "handmaiden." Naturally, this comparison plays on something of an equivocation on the term *science*. Still, Locke served as a preeminent advocate for a new conception of philosophy and knowledge alike. Of course, not all philosophers have shared Locke's enthusiasm for the relegation of their discipline. And while those assaying to grasp the history of language may have largely agreed on the etymological facts, they have not all seen in them support for Locke's empiricist epistemology. Ralph Waldo Emerson, for instance, offered a dissenting interpretation of the evidence at hand when he cited the same trend in support of something much closer to Aquinas's view than to Locke's. In *Nature*, he sets forth a vision which might best be characterized as an inspired pantheism:

> Every word which is used to express a moral or intellectual fact, if traced to its root, is found to be borrowed from some material appearance. Right means straight; wrong means twisted. Spirit primarily means wind; transgression, the crossing of a line; supercilious, the raising of the eyebrow. We say the heart to express emotion, the head to denote thought; and thought and emotion are words borrowed from sensible things, and now appropriated to spiritual nature.[14]

Emerson concluded that the apparent homogeneity of language and nature, as evinced by the seeming emergence of one from the other, indicates an actual correspondence between them. For him, language and nature were two rivers flowing from a common transcendent source. "Every natural fact is a symbol of some spiritual fact," Emerson affirmed, and "language" itself—especially poetic or "picturesque" language—"is proper creation. It is the working of the Original Cause through the instruments he has already made."[15] Hence, the medieval conflict between realism and nominalism can

---

14. Emerson, "Nature," Ch. IV.

15. Emerson, "Nature," Ch. IV. Though Emerson is not often acknowledged with Goethe, Coleridge, and Steiner as a major influence on Barfield's work, some of the affinities between Barfield and Emerson are striking. Carol and Philip Zaleski noted this in *Fellowship*: "[O]ne may note that Emerson declared in 'The Poet' that 'language is the archives of history,' and in 'In Praise of Books' that dictionaries are 'the raw material of possible poems and histories,' and one wonders about the extent of his influence on Barfield, largely unacknowledged apart from scattered references in the latter's 1931 *Poetic Diction* and a few essays." *Fellowship*, 106. Most notable of these scattered references is the acknowledgment at the end of *Poetic Diction*, where Barfield says that Emerson's

be rediscovered, transformed and transposed to an early modern intellectual environment, in the diverging views of Emerson and Locke, respectively.

Despite disagreements between these philosophers, and among many
others, about the ultimate significance of the fact that "[t]hroughout the
recorded history of language, the movement of meaning has been from
concrete to abstract,"[16] this basic proposition tended to serve as a kind of
invariable fulcrum around which Barfield's predecessors leveraged their arguments.[17] Indeed, a broad consensus had emerged by the early nineteenth
century, and even found relatively popular expression in the work of Max
Müller, on the following propositions, which, taken together in sequence,
will be referred to henceforth as "the received view":

1. Languages were originally composed almost entirely of words that
   referred exclusively to particular, concrete, sensible objects.

2. As humans developed the capacity for reason, the need arose to express increasingly general, abstract, and insensible ideas. Since such
   ideas have no sensible referents and since, *ex hypothesi*, all language
   derives from such referents, ancient humans simply "poured the new
   wine in the old wineskins" and repurposed existing words to new ends.

3. a. This process of repurposing was accomplished through the deliberate use of metaphor or simile.

   b. The above is a likely story given that the historical record allows
   us to observe comparatively recent instances of such formations (e.g,
   "perspective," the Latinate form of "point-of-view" referred to a literal
   standpoint in space until Coleridge enlisted the term to refer to cognitive "space").

4. When this metaphorical transposition of a particular, concrete,
   sensible referent was successful—that is, when the expression was
   understood—the metaphorical meaning was employed to the point
   of becoming a cliché until finally its metaphorical origin was all but

---

dictum "Language is fossil poetry" is "a flash of insight which covers practically all that
has been written in these pages." *Poetic Diction,* 179.

16. Barfield, *Saving the Appearances,* 117.

17. Many other examples could be given. Jeremy Bentham, for instance, appealed
to the apparent origin of all language in material references in support of his proto-
positivist philosophy: "Throughout the whole field of language, parallel to the line of
what may be termed the material language, and expressed by the same words, runs a
line of what may be termed the immaterial language. Not that every word that has a
material import there belongs also an immaterial one; but that to every word that has
an immaterial import, there belongs, or at least did belong, a material one." Bentham,
"Essay on Language," 329.

forgotten and the abstract referent came to entirely displace the original meaning. By this process, general, abstract, and insensible meanings were gradually interpolated into ancient languages.

5. As noted above, the original particular, concrete, sensible meaning would ultimately be forgotten, resulting in the high proportion of words with purely abstract meanings, so common in modern languages.

Thus, from the fact that almost any word can be traced to an earlier time in which it referred to one kind of thing, post-nominalist thinkers from Locke's time onward increasingly drew the inference that current words that refer to a different kind of thing were appropriated for this task through a deliberate application of metaphor. By the time Barfield arrived on the scene, the above had been accepted as a general consensus. In his words: "one of the first things that a student of etymology—even quite an amateur student—discovers for himself is that every modern language, with its thousands of abstract terms and its nuances of meaning and association, is *apparently* nothing, from beginning to end, but an unconscionable tissue of dead, or petrified metaphors."[18]

According to Barfield, however, the received view in respect to the origin and phylogeny of language is less a case of reasoning from evidence to theory than of assuming a foregone theory at the outset and then selectively gathering and assembling evidence to rationalize it *post hoc*. To wit, the premises on which the received view was established receive scant support from direct historical study of language itself. Instead, thinkers appeared to tacitly assume these premises at the outset of their inquiry as a function of the broader paradigm in which their research transpired. The proposed evidence for the received view was derived not through direct investigation into the question at hand, but from a larger structure of beliefs, almost universally held, about the content and character of the ancient mind, and the general trajectory of its development. These views on the ancient mind ("that luckless dustbin of pseudo-scientific fantasies"), Barfield argued, were drawn from disciplines other than the historical study of language itself. This displacement of support had the effect of promulgating a tendentious view of the origin of language and thereby of foreclosing *bona fide* research in the field best suited to offer real insight into the matter at hand. Moreover, it also foreclosed the best—and arguably the only—window of insight into the inner lives of people in prior ages. In Barfield's estimation, this window was none other than the evolution of language, correctly grasped. Conclusions about linguistic and semantic history, then, should be drawn from

18. Barfield, *Poetic Diction*, 63. (Barfield's emphasis.)

linguistic and semantic evidence and, in turn, one's understanding of the content and character of the ancient mind should be formed, at least largely, on the basis of such conclusions.

What, then, did Barfield discover when he peered through the window of the evolution of language and into the content and character of the ancient mind? The received view had postulated a derivation of immaterial meanings from material references by means of metaphor. Barfield asserts, to the contrary, that the notions of both "materiality" and its contrary alike result from a process of semantic polarization that separated out these two categories of meaning from an anterior unity that encompassed them both in an undifferentiated condition. In other words, materiality and immateriality are not contrarieties so much as complementarities. To suggest, therefore, that language began with purely material import and gradually expanded its scope to include immaterial extensions is an anachronism akin to arguing that Ovid was a Romantic poet. It is, in fact, a particularly subtle and pernicious kind of anachronism in which present states of consciousness are read into prior states of consciousness. Since changes in consciousness were one of Barfield's primary concerns, he coined a useful term for this kind of anachronism: "logomorphism." One of the benefits of reading Barfield's work is the manner in which it fosters an increased awareness of this pervasive and fallacious habit of thought with the result that one is less inclined to fall into it.

Barfield illustrated his view of the ancient semantic unity in language with the example of the modern English words *spirit* and *soul*. In many ancient languages, the words that appear in modern English translation as either *spirit* or *soul* are also said to mean both "breath" or "wind." One may consider, for instance, the connection between such words as *spirit, inspiration, respiration, expiration,* and *suspiration*, mediated via the Latin root *spiritus*, to see this connection (we will find occasion to return to the word *soul* in a later chapter). On the received view, this fact could be, and has often been, explained in something like the following manner: ancient people had, to begin with, only a vague and inarticulate conception of soul and spirit. As the human mind increased in its capacity for abstraction and figurative thought, the ideas of *soul* and *spirit* became sufficiently well-defined in the minds of select persons. As a result, they began looking for a word to express their budding conception. Naturally, a tangible and publicly accessible image was needed. Because of a dim isomorphism that was intimated between the concept of *spirit* and the perception of *breath* and *wind*, the latter managed to effectively suggest the former and were adapted as metaphors. The material referents of these metaphors gradually fell into disuse as suitable substitutes were found (i.e., *breath, wind*), and this left *soul* and *spirit* to designate the purely intangible meanings. Hence the presence of what seems to be a double meaning in most ancient languages.

In contrast, Barfield offers a different account of how the meanings encoded in modern languages came about. In his words:

> the study of the history of meaning . . . assures us that such a purely material content as "wind," on the one hand, and on the other, such a purely abstract content as "the principle of life within man or animal" are both late arrivals in the human consciousness. Their abstractness and their simplicity are alike evidence of long ages of intellectual evolution. So far from the psychic meaning of "spiritus" having arisen because someone had the abstract idea, "principle of life . . ." and wanted a word for it, the abstract idea "principle of life" is itself a product of the old concrete meaning "spiritus," which contained within itself the germs of both later significations. We must therefore imagine a time when "spiritus" or (*pneuma*), or spirit, nor yet all three of these things, but when they simply had their own old peculiar meaning, which has since, in the course of the evolution of consciousness, crystallized into the three meanings.[19]

Barfield further illustrates the contrast between the received view and his own view (which, according to C. S. Lewis, Tolkien helpfully called the "theory of ancient semantic unity") by pointing his reader to a text from the Gospel of John.[20] On the received view, the Evangelist was employing the term *pneuma* equivocally when he wrote that

> The wind [*pneuma*] bloweth where it listeth, and thou hearest the sound thereof, but canst not tell whence it cometh, and whither it goeth: so is every one that is born of the Spirit [*pneuma*].

In the first instance, the word is often supposed to be a literal reference to wind. Hence, "the [*pneuma*] bloweth where it listeth, and thou hearest the sound thereof." In the second instance, *pneuma* is supposed to refer, by way of metaphor, to that which is meant by the English word *spirit* (including, in this instance, the personal and theological overtones that come with the translator's use of a definite article and capital "S"). The term *pneuma* as rendered in the phrase "everyone born of the Spirit," is therefore understood to indicate something different than the *pneuma* that "bloweth where

19. Barfield, *Poetic Diction*, 80–81.
20. John 3:8.

it listeth." Hence the Evangelist's use of the term *pneuma* is interpreted as decidedly equivocal, and presumably metaphorical.

On Barfield's account, however, the Evangelist's use of the term *pneuma* (in this instance and many others) is univocal. The *pneuma* that bloweth where it listeth and the *pneuma* whence a man may be born again is the same *pneuma*. Hence, Barfield maintains that the Evangelist did not compose a sentence that is patently ambiguous or fancifully figurative. He instead employed this term deliberately and univocally to convey a meaning that the modern mind finds difficult to grasp and virtually impossible to express. At the time when the Gospel of John was written (ca. first century), Barfield argues, the word retained a largely undivided meaning that was neither purely material nor purely immaterial.[21] The compulsion for modern translators to employ two English words *wind* and *spirit* for a single Greek one arises not from the original author's equivocal use of the term, but as a result of fundamental changes in the meanings of words that are, in turn, a reflection of the evolution of consciousness. The conceptual distinctions that are naturalized in modern English express meanings that characterize a different state of consciousness than that of the author of the Gospel of John. In general, it may be observed that the thoughts and the expressions characteristic of modern English forfeit in *fullness* what they gain in *precision*; English words are at once less rich and more exact than their ancient Greek counterparts—a thesis that accords with the trajectory of development from ancient languages to modern ones more generally. Let us observe, however, that while phenomena of a certain kind will be more amenable to conceptualization by way of precision, others may be rendered decidedly unintelligible for the same reason that analyzing a text with an electron microscope makes it virtually impossible to read. Any movement of precision or analysis represents a departure from the prior whole to which all of those analytical elements pertain. If the departure is too extreme or too sustained, a resulting obliviousness to the wholeness is likely to incur. Indeed, Barfield suggests that this is precisely what has occurred in respect to modern consciousness when he observes that the original meaning of *pneuma* "and therefore, in this case, practically the whole sense of the passage . . . is lost in the inevitably double English rendering of spirit . . . and wind."[22]

---

21. Barfield notes that some words, like "heart," still faintly embody an old semantic unity. Though we can easily distinguish between the physical and psychical meanings of "heart," we are still strongly inclined to associate the emotions with the chest, despite having no physiological justification for doing so.

22. Barfield, *Poetic Diction*, 80. Cf. David Bentley Hart: "If we could hear the language of πνεῦμα [pneuma, spirit] with late antique ears, our sense of the text's meaning would not be that of two utterly distinct concepts—one "physical" and one "mystical"—only

The above discussion of the Greek word *pneuma* and its apparently equivocal usage in a single passage is but one of myriad instances in which the interpretative standards of modern readers lead them inadvertently to misconstrue ancient authors in their attempts at translation. The New Testament is comparatively recent and yet Barfield indicates just how susceptible a modern reader is to be tripped up by construing an equivocation when the original meaning was undivided. Commenting on the term *pneuma*, Hart observes that it is like other crucial terms such as *logos* and *psyche* in that "there is no single English equivalent of the word that could possibly comprise the full range of its connotations and nuances." He goes on to say that:

> [t]he inevitable result of this . . . as is the case in any translation of a conceptually rich . . . term, is that what appeared to the author of the original to be a complex but coherent unity of meaning becomes for the translator, and those dependent on his or her labors, a cloud of associations—or, really, of dissociations.[23]

From this insight, Hart enunciates a characteristically Barfieldian principle to guide translations, especially of older texts: "[W]hat the original author considered a conceptual unity the translator should not try to convert into a multiplicity of distinct concepts."[24] Unfortunately, the translator is often left with no choice but to employ discrete terms, for the contemporary connotations of these words have condensed and fallen asunder to such a degree that their prior unities are perceptible only with great effort, a straining of the inner faculties to discern the faint traces of resemblance. The attempt to hearken back to a prior univocity between what to our eyes appear as manifestly distinct phenomena is unlikely to be undertaken spontaneously, and it would thus make little sense for contemporary translators to follow Hart's counsel unless their readers had internalized Hart's principle of translation into a principle of hermeneutics as well. We hope that the present

---

metaphorically entangled with one another by dint of a verbal equivocity; rather, we would almost surely hear only a single concept expressed univocally through a single word, a concept in which the physical and the mystical would remain undifferentiated." From "Spiritual Was More Substantial Than the Material for the Ancients."

23. Hart, "Concluding Scientific Postscript," 560–61. Of the lack of adequate translation of λόγος, Barfield had this to say: "[T]here is really no way of translating words like λόγος, λογικός, λογίζεσθαι, as they are used by Plato. *Reason* is quite inadequate to convey to a twentieth-century imagination the cosmic process which Plato must have felt to be taking place—as much out in the world and among the stars as "within" his own mind—when he spoke of τὸ λογιστικόν or contrasted νοῦς and ἐπιστήμη with δόξα. It was not until the 'analytic' method of thought arose with Aristotle that such a word as *logic* could begin to take on its modern meaning." From "Greek Thought in English Words."

24. Hart, "Concluding Scientific Postscript," 561.

exposition may contribute to this end, thereby equipping contemporary readers to encounter ancient texts on terms that are closer to their own. The alternative is of course a sort of Procrustean approach to hermeneutics, in which we force original meanings to fit contemporary molds. In view of this, after summarizing Barfield's findings about the historical development of language, Lewis drew the following conclusion about its significance: "As long as we are trying to read back into that ancient unity either the one or the other of the two opposites which have since been analysed out of it, we shall misread all early literature and ignore many states of consciousness which we ourselves still from time to time experience. The point is crucial not only for the present discussion but for any sound literary criticism or philosophy."[25]

25. Lewis, *Miracles*, 369. See all of chapter 7 for Lewis's engagement with and application of Barfield's theory of ancient semantic unity.

3

Poetry

INTENSIVE MEDITATION ON THE history of language brought Barfield to the insight that the basic character of ancient consciousness was markedly different than had generally been supposed. Old words, he realized, represent fossilized forms of earlier states of consciousness. To the one who is able to read them, these fossils testify that the physical and psychical worlds were inextricably intertwined in the minds of ancient people. This realization compelled Barfield to question the commonplace view of consciousness, which has so often been taken for granted (at least in modern times): to wit, that consciousness is, and has always been, a passive recipient of impressions caused by purely physical objects. Many of Barfield's findings in respect to the nature of poetry, which will be explored in this chapter, further corroborated his skepticism about the conventional theory of consciousness and led him, ultimately, to propose an alternative, which will be the subject of the chapters to follow.

Though poetry itself is at least as old as civilization, theories of poetry—theories, that is, about the nature, function, and value of poetry—can only be traced back as far as ancient Greece. Plato's writings, for instance, bear the rudiments of a theory of poetry which can be seen in his concern about the moral effects it has on the young, his doctrine of *mimesis,* and his understanding of *inspiration* as the process by which poetry is produced.[1] It was Plato's student Aristotle, however, who first attempted a somewhat

1. For Plato's understanding of inspiration, see *Ion.* For his doctrine of mimesis, see books II, III, and X of *Republic.*

systematic treatment of the subject.[2] Many poets, critics, and philosophers since Aristotle's time have made similar attempts by conducting inquiries into questions about the source of poetry, the phenomenology of poetic experience, the distinction between poetic and prosaic language, and the criteria by which instances of poetry are judged to be good or bad. What makes the subject interesting is that there has been, at least in the West, relatively widespread agreement about the *extension* of the term (i.e., what instances of literature count as instances of poetry, good or bad), despite the fact that theories of poetry, which are primarily concerned with the *intension* of the term, are fraught with differences. Hence, when Boswell asked Dr. Johnson "Sir, what is poetry?" Johnson replied as follows: "Why, Sir, it is much easier to say what it is not. We all *know* what light is; but it is not easy to *tell* what it is."[3]

Nevertheless, despite his original intentions to the contrary, Barfield ended up attempting to "tell what it is." But we will not here try to summarize Barfield's answer. Such a summary would be nothing more or less than a restatement of the content of *Poetic Diction,* which would inevitably fail to do justice to that rich and endlessly suggestive text. In this instance, an adequate reiteration of Barfield's argument would of necessity be nearly coextensive with the argument itself and a map that is identical with the territory that it seeks to represent is not much use. What will follow, then, is an analysis of certain aspects of Barfield's theory of poetry that serve to advance the general progress of this book, namely, elements of Barfield's theory of poetry that are germane to his theory of the evolution of consciousness.

The first issue to be addressed, in keeping with Dr. Johnson's suggestion, is "what [poetry] is not." While it is clear that all poetry is conveyed by means of language, it is just as clear that not all language is poetic; saying otherwise is akin to equating music and noise. Though it is not obvious where the line between poetic and prosaic language should be drawn, it is important to note that Barfield stands with the majority of critics who recognize that

2. Thus Aristotle begins *Poetics* with the following words: "I propose to treat of Poetry in itself and of its various kinds, noting the essential quality of each, to inquire into the structure of the plot as requisite to a good poem; into the number and nature of the parts of which a poem is composed; and similarly into whatever else falls within the same inquiry."

3. Boswell, *Life of Johnson,* 744. Despite his hesitancy in this context, Johnson confidently offered an answer to this question in the essay on Milton in *Lives of Poets*: "Poetry is the art of uniting pleasure with truth, by calling imagination to the help of reason." *Lives of Poets,* 100.

the distinction between *poetic* and *prosaic* language is *not* the same as the simpler and clearer distinction between *verse* and *prose*. As Barfield noted, "This artificial identification of the words *poetry* and *poetic* with metrical form is certainly long standing in popular use; but it has rarely been supported by those who have written on the subject."[4]

The popular association between poetry and structured verse is dubious on *conceptual* as well as *historical* grounds. It is *conceptually* dubious because it fails to account for the wide agreement among poets and critics, mentioned above, concerning literary works that are clear instances of poetry, but are not written in verse, and instances of verse that are clearly not poetic; only a philistine would hold that "prosaic verse" or "poetic prose" are essentially oxymorons. The equation is, moreover, *historically* dubious because it rests on an invalid inference from correlation to identity. A strong correlation can indeed be observed in the history of literature between verse and poetry but it does not follow that the two are therefore identical. Indeed, if one does look back, especially into ancient literature, it will be difficult to find poetry that is not metrical, but this is because, in Barfield's words, "All literatures are, in their infancy, metrical, that is to say, based on a more or less regularly recurring rhythm."[5] To extrapolate, however, this historical datum to the present is akin to affirming that a flower never differentiates from its calyx or that material objects are identical with their position in space. Diachronic consideration reveals material divergence in the first case and synchronic consideration provides for conceptual differentiation in the second—every object *occupies* a position but no object *is* that position. In the same way, poetry can be shown both to depart from its identification with verse through history as well as to present an energetic function of language that cannot be invoked on purely formal grounds. Thus, "those writers who have seriously set out to discuss and define poetry have very rarely made metre their criterion, yet, *for historical reasons,* most of the poetry with which they have actually had to deal has, in fact, been in metrical form; and it is this, in all probability, which has given rise to the terminological confusion."[6]

Despite the fact that meter is not interchangeable with poetry, the historical ascendency of prose (in this case, nonmetrical writing) is, nonetheless, a noteworthy phenomenon, which has long perplexed philologists and

---

4. Barfield, *Poetic Diction,* 145. Barfield was aware, of course, that there are a few exceptions. Hegel, for instance, regarded the "versification" of language as the criterion for poetry. Before him there was Francis Bacon, who identified "verse" as one sense of the term "poetry," though not the only or most important sense.

5. Barfield, *Poetic Diction,* 156–57.

6. Barfield, *Poetic Diction,* 146.

historians of literature. One common explanation is that preliterate societies passed on stories and information orally, and verse was used almost exclusively because it was easier to commit to memory. Eventually, as cultures developed systems for writing, the oral tradition was condensed into written form, so most early literature is transcribed verse. While this account is undoubtedly plausible, Barfield believed that it was far from sufficient as a comprehensive explanation of the phenomenon in question, not the least because it lacks firm evidential support and, moreover, because it relies on a fallacy that Barfield termed "logomorphism," which is the tendency to retroject present states of consciousness into prior ones and thence to interpret them in a light that is not their own.

Another noteworthy factor that may have conspired to bring about the migration of literature from meter to prose is the observable and seemingly inevitable progress commonly observed in languages from "syntheticity" to "analyticity." Highly synthetic languages, like ancient Greek and Latin, are heavily inflected. This is to say that they use declensions and conjugations to indicate the grammatical function of a word in a sentence. As a result, the order of words in heavily inflected languages is fluid and a single word may wear many hats, as it were, according to the company in which it finds itself. The grammatical function of a word in an analytic language, by contrast, remains largely fixed and is determined, for the most part, by the place it occupies in a sentence. Synthetic languages are more conducive to verse than analytic languages because of the former's more flexible word order and the relatively small number of endings that are applied to every noun and verb. The result is that both rhythm and rhyme precipitate more naturally in a synthetic language than an analytic one. Trading morphological complexity for syntactic complexity, analytic languages require much more work and ingenuity on the part of the individual writer to adequately convey his or her meaning without violating metrical constraints to the one side and grammatical ones to the other. Fixed word order and a general lack of repeated endings make the composition of verse exceedingly difficult. As Western culture has developed, spoken languages have become increasingly analytic. It stands to reason, then, that the waning of verse and the rise of prose, which can be observed in the history of Western literature, correlates to the process by which languages lose their heavily inflected structure. Still, though, Barfield was not satisfied with such a purely correlational explanation for the late ascendency of prose. Ultimately, he thought, an explanation must be offered that goes beyond construing this shift as a historical accident. Instead, Barfield sought an explanation that could disclose the historical coherence and even necessity of this transition, which he found in the evolution of human consciousness through history.

One way of characterizing the evolution of consciousness, which will be treated more thoroughly in the chapters to follow, is that it is the process by which the consciousness of earlier eras has developed into its familiar modern forms, which are set apart from preceding forms by a high degree of "subjectivity" or self-consciousness. Before the rise of self-consciousness, Barfield argued, human beings participated in the life of nature in a way that modern people are unable, except in rare moments, to do. "Objectively," Barfield said,

> we could only describe the earlier stages of this process as a time when man—not only as a body, but also as a soul—was a part of nature in a way which we today, of course, find it difficult to conceive. Subjectively, he could not yet "call his soul his own." The farther back we penetrate, the more indistinguishable would his acts and utterances become from processes taking place in . . . "nature."[7]

In general, human beings no longer consciously participate in the life of nature, but self-consciously observe this life as outsiders. For Barfield, an essential ingredient in the distinct pleasure of poetry, as we shall see, is the recovery of some small part of this ancient participation through the use of fitting metaphors, which suggest forgotten connections between our inner life and the outer world. These metaphors, each in their own way, free one's thinking from the detached mental world of abstract thoughts, and renew the lost sense of participation that makes apprehension of meaning in nature possible.

For this reason, Barfield described early literature, especially the mythologies of primitive cultures, as something more like "nature speaking through man" than "man speaking through nature."[8] As an explanation for the increasing dominance of verse in older literature, Barfield proposed that primitive verse represents a state of consciousness that obtained at a time before abstract thought and self-consciousness fully emerged from an instinctive participation in the life and rhythms of nature. Today, by contrast, we are wont to confront nature as passive spectators: "we are obliged to assume that the verse-rhythms were 'given' by Nature in the same way as the earliest 'meanings.' And this is comprehensible enough. Nature herself is perpetually rhythmic."[9] Barfield goes on to say that

7. Barfield, *Saving the Appearances*, 123.
8. Barfield, *Poetic Diction*, 157.
9. Barfield, *Poetic Diction*, 157.

[j]ust as the myths still live on in ghostly life as fables after they have died as real meaning, so the old rhythmic consciousness of Nature (it should rather be called *participation* than a consciousness) lives on as the tradition of metrical form. We can only understand the origin of metre by going back to the ages when men were conscious, not merely in their heads, but in the beating of their hearts and the pulsing of their blood—when thinking was not merely *of* Nature, but was Nature herself.[10]

This is the point at which verse and poetry are closely associated. Though they are not synonymous, verse can add poetic value to words because of its ability to rekindle something in the mind of its recipient that has been extinguished in the process by which youthful language has lignified into prose and human consciousness has evolved into its onlooker mode. In Barfield's words,

> The very fact that his rhythms have a high poetic value should now suggest to us that the poet, while creating anew, is likely to be in a sense restoring something old. And of the most ancient rhythms of verse are but the sound, dying away, of just those "footsteps of Nature" whose visible print we have observed . . . in the present possibility of true metaphor, we shall hardly be surprised to hear in the music which such a poet creates, albeit spontaneously, something like an echo of just those rhythms.[11]

In addition to the claim that poetry is distinct from verse, Barfield makes another point that may seem obvious, but is, nonetheless, important: "[Poetry] is not merely so many waves in the air or ink marks on a piece of paper."[12] And also: "Whatever poetry may be . . . it is something more than the signs or sounds by which it is conveyed."[13] Barfield's investigation, then, is not primarily concerned with anything in the "outer world," which is to

10. Barfield, *Poetic Diction*, 157.

11. Barfield, *Poetic Diction*, 158. Of course, other writers have made similar observations. John Dewey, for instance, looked at the historical development of art and identified the way in which it arises from (or, should arise from) direct experience of the natural cycles and rhythms of nature and of human life, conceived not as something separate from the natural world, but as a part of nature itself. He also noted the fact that in earlier ages art, including poetry, arose naturally from humanity's direct experience which was, more so than now, an experience of complete dependence upon, and intimate connection with, the rhythms of the natural world. See *Art as Experience*, 153–55.

12. Barfield, *Poetic Diction*, 41.

13. Barfield, *Poetic Diction*, 41.

say, anything that lends itself directly to measurement or quantification by scientific means. The beginning and the end of poetry is in the "inner world" of consciousness and its passage through the outer world is only a means. This point is important, among other reasons, because it justifies the seriousness with which Barfield takes his own aesthetic experiences and those of the critics he engages: "To the genuine critic," he says "the spiritual fact of his own aesthetic experience, when once he knows inwardly that it is purged of all personal affectation, must have at least equal weight with any reported historical or scientific facts which may be placed beside it."[14] Poetic knowledge (i.e., the kind of knowledge that poetry uniquely embodies or conveys) is to be sought by the same means that all knowledge is sought, for the goal is "to reconcile or relate conceptually all the elements included in [a person's] perceptual experience."[15] Most people will immediately think of seeking coherence among the objects of material perception; when it comes to poetry, "aesthetic reactions" must also be included in the process of reconciliation.[16]

Barfield was also aware, of course, that the aesthetic reactions of any particular individual are not themselves sufficient grounds upon which a comprehensive theory of poetry can be built. If poetry is to be a source of anything other than knowledge of one's own psychology, it must be possible to formulate some objective principles by which instances of poetry can be recognized and evaluated. He went out of his way to make this point because, at the time of his writing, theorists and critics of literature were beginning to put a much greater emphasis on both the subjective feelings of the poet and the subjective responses of his or her readers, thereby reducing criticism to speculations on the idiosyncrasies of an individual poet or reader's psychology. Thus, Barfield clarifies both the method and goal of his investigation:

> In view . . . of the predominantly personal direction taken by literary criticism during the last few decades, it may be well to point out here that to *start* with personal experience does not

14. Barfield, *Poetic Diction*, 70. This point was especially important at the time when Barfield was writing. In his day, the most influential literary critic in the English-speaking world was I. A. Richards. Richards rejected the common antithesis between "poetic" and "prosaic" language in favor of an antithesis between "poetic" and "scientific" language. His ultimate conclusion was that scientific language communicates truth because it refers to the real world, whereas poetic language has no truth-value because it has no reference; it is merely emotive. Barfield criticizes Richards's distinction in "Language and Discovery," in *Rediscovery of Meaning and Other Essays*, 157.

15. Barfield, *Poetic Diction*, 70.

16. Barfield, *Poetic Diction*, 70.

necessarily mean to finish with it. One may start from direct, personal, aesthetic experience without prejudice to the possibility of arriving in the end at some objective standards of criticism—standards that a young critic might set before himself as an aid to the elimination of just those personal affectations and associations—the accidents rather than the substance of poetry—which are always at hand to distort his judgement.[17]

As stated above, it was not Barfield's original intention to formulate a full-fledged theory of poetry. All he really wished to do was provide something more modest and less philosophical: that is, a theory of poetic diction. In other words, he wished simply to identify words and grammatical constructions that are associated with poetry, and to explain why they are generally perceived as poetic rather than prosaic. A theory of poetic diction, Barfield suggested, should do little more than explain why the phrase "prophets old" is considered poetic, while the phrase "old prophets," would be more naturally at home in prose.[18] How, then, did Barfield define poetic diction, and why did this definition force him to formulate a more wide-ranging theory of poetry? Barfield's initial take on this question was fairly straightforward: "When words are selected and arranged in a way that their meaning either arouses, or is obviously intended to arouse, aesthetic imagination, the result may be described as *poetic diction*."[19] This may not, at first sight, appear to be an improvement on Coleridge's vague and unsatisfying description of poetry as "the best words in the best order," but Barfield allowed himself a way forward in his investigation of what the phenomenology of poetic experience reveals about poetry itself by including the phrase "arouses, or is obviously intended to arouse, aesthetic imagination." It was Barfield's attempt to elucidate this phrase that compelled him to bring a broader theory of poetry into play.

So what does Barfield conclude about the arousal of the aesthetic imagination, on the basis of his own inner experiences associated with the reading of poetry? Barfield analyzed his own experience as follows: "I find myself obliged to define it as a 'felt change of consciousness,' where 'consciousness' embraces all my awareness of my surroundings at any given moment, and 'surroundings' includes my own feelings."[20] This felt change of

17. Barfield, *Poetic Diction*, 15.
18. Barfield, *Poetic Diction*, 41.
19. Barfield, *Poetic Diction*, 41.
20. Barfield, *Poetic Diction*, 48.

consciousness is, for Barfield, the paradigm of poetic experience and insofar as words have the power to bring it about, those words may be counted as poetic.[21] What Barfield has in mind is something more than the mere acquisition of new information about the world; it is, rather, a fundamental and qualitative shift in one's relation to the world that affects how one perceives, experiences, and ultimately understands it. Poetry, in this sense, and in the words of Thoreau, may be said "to carve and paint the very atmosphere and medium through which we look" and, for this reason, must be classed as "the highest of arts."[22] The lasting effect of this change includes a person's possession of a larger, richer, and more unified conception of the world.[23]

Barfield observed that the most common and easily identifiable means by which aesthetic imagination is aroused, bringing about felt changes in consciousness, is through encounters with figurative language, especially metaphors, which are often taken to be a *sine qua non* of poetic expression.[24] As so many poets and theorists have noted, metaphor is not merely an ornament to speech and writing, or a way of illustrating an idea. On the contrary, true metaphor is the source of meaning in language. Language is essentially and ineluctably metaphorical in that words are always conveying meanings. Hence, metaphor represents an intensification or second-order function of what language embodies in its very being. The best metaphors, Barfield argued, reveal actual connections between the material and immaterial, or the physical and psychical worlds, thereby lending greater coherence to a person's perception and understanding. In other words, the function of

---

21. Of course, there are counterfeit experiences that do not amount to the "felt change of consciousness" that Barfield here describes. They may be associated with words, and they may bring pleasure or insight, but the pleasure and insight they bring is not specifically poetic. Further, the absence of a felt change of consciousness, in any particular case, does not entail a lack of poetry. The absence may be due to the insensibility of the reader or the state of consciousness in which the words were read.

22. Thoreau, *Walden, Civil Disobedience and Other Writings*, 65.

23. One obvious implication of this, mentioned in passing above, is that one word or group of words is going to be more or less poetic depending on the state of a the reader's consciousness in relation to the poet's. Indeed, for this reason, a poet's words may be experienced as poetic for some and not at all for others. Barfield is careful, however, to point out that this does not lead to relativism about poetic values, for certain groups of words may have a much greater propensity to bring about a change in consciousness than others, even if the nature and extent of the change itself is relative to each individual's state of consciousness at the time they encounter the instance of poetry in question. This is why Barfield felt it important to include a warning about "the predominantly personal direction" in which much literary criticism was tending in his time, and has continued to tend since.

24. Barfield, "Owen Barfield and the Origin of Language."

figurative language is epistemic, not merely aesthetic or heuristic.[25] Poetic metaphors can arouse the aesthetic imagination by fittingly pairing general and abstract notions with particular and concrete images, not only *illuminating* ideas, but *incarnating* them. Such images, aptly employed, bridge the gap between the material and immaterial, lending vitality to the former and the comprehensibility to the latter. Part of poetry's power, then, is in its ability to pierce the veil of abstraction that, according to Barfield, is hung between the modern mind and the phenomenal world. For it is, on Barfield's view, a distinctive condition of modern consciousness to be partitioned from the appearances of nature by the curtain of its own abstract concepts.[26]

Barfield also noticed, however, that the "felt change of consciousness" can sometimes be occasioned by language that is not overtly figurative, much less metaphorical. Ancient languages, in particular, very often bear an intrinsically poetic quality. The reason for this is clear in light of Barfield's discoveries, discussed in chapter 2, in respect to the development of modern language from earlier stages; stages in which the boundary between abstract and concrete, material and immaterial, or subjective and objective meanings remained less distinct. Though they are not themselves metaphors, the semantic unities that were encoded as simple, "given" meanings in ancient languages ultimately serve to evoke the same "felt change in consciousness" as metaphor because they both serve to disclose, in one's consciousness "the hitherto unapprehended relations of things," whose connection was sundered by the polarization of experience into the oppositions indicated above.[27] For Barfield, then, one important function of poetry—a function

25. See Barfield, "On the Meaning of Literal," in *Rediscovery of Meaning and Other Essays*. This is what C. S. Lewis meant when he spoke of a "psycho-physical parallelism" in the world (see passage quoted in the discussion of the "Great War" in chapter 1). Emerson affirmed this as well in "Nature," where he said that "[i]t is not words only that are emblematic; it is things which are emblematic. Every natural fact is a symbol of some spiritual fact." Thus, like Barfield, Emerson's reflection on the development of language led to his belief that there is a "radical correspondence between visible things and human thoughts." Ch. IV.

26. Cf. Emerson: "Hundreds of writers may be found in every long-civilized nation, who for a short time believe, and make others believe, that they see and utter truths, who do not of themselves clothe one thought in its natural garment." Such are seen by those with some poetic sensibility to be imitating poetic genius rather than possessing genius themselves. They "feed unconsciously on the language created by the primary writers of the country, those, namely, who hold primarily on nature." "Nature," Ch. IV.

27. Barfield, then, disagreed with Shelley who, in the context of his discussion of the role of figurative language in poetry, wrote that metaphorical language "marks the before unapprehended relations of things and perpetuates their apprehension, until the words which represent them, become, through time, signs for portions or classes of thoughts instead of pictures of integral thoughts." According to Barfield, this was not the whole truth: "it is the language of the poets, in so far as they create true metaphors,

that has become increasingly important over the course of history—is to restore and preserve unity to perception and thought: "The world, like Dionysus, is torn to pieces by pure intellect; but the poet is Zeus; he has swallowed the heart of the world; and he can reproduce it as a living body."[28]

As before, Barfield found poetic values to be rooted in the power of words, properly selected and arranged, to restore an older form of consciousness, one in which the human mind participated more in the life of nature. Thus, alluding to a passage in Bacon's *Advancement of Learning*, Barfield wrote that it is the "'footsteps of nature' whose noise we hear alike in primitive language and in the finest metaphors of the poets." He goes on to spell out what this insight, along with the discoveries he made about the development of language, seem to imply about absolute dependence of all knowledge on the idea of "true metaphor," which has already been alluded to, though not explained: "Men do not *invent* those mysterious relations," he argued, "between separate external objects, and between objects and feelings or ideas, which it is the function of poetry to reveal. These relations exist independently, not indeed of Thought, but of any individual thinker."[29] Not only do they exist independently of any individual thinker, but these relations were once immediately perceived, not metaphorically, but immediately and concretely. C. S. Lewis summarized Barfield's understanding of the matter in the following passage from *The Allegory of Love*:

> It is of the very nature of thought and language to represent what is immaterial in picturable terms. What is good or happy has always been high like the heavens and bright like the sun. Evil and misery were deep and dark from the first. Pain is black in Homer, and goodness is a middle point for Alfred no less than for Aristotle. To ask how these married pairs of sensibles and insensibles first came together would be great folly; the real question is how they ever came apart.[30]

Barfield's understanding of poetry and its relation to language and consciousness at various points in their development has many further

---

which must restore this unity conceptually, after it has been lost from perception. Thus, the before-apprehended relationships of which Shelley spoke, are in a sense forgotten relationships. For though they were never yet apprehended, they were at one time seen. And imagination can see them again." *Poetic Diction,* 87.

28. Barfield, *Poetic Diction,* 88.

29. Barfield, *Poetic Diction,* 86.

30. Lewis, *Allegory of Love,* 55–56.

implications, only one more of which may be noted here. From what has been said so far, it will be clear that in Barfield's view, people once unconsciously drew meaning from nature in the same way that we draw breath from the atmosphere. Perceptions were once pregnant with meaning and the poet needed only lend his voice to become, in a sense, the mouthpiece of the gods, muses, or elemental spirits. Because of this, language itself *was* poetry. As a result of changes in the configuration of consciousness, however, the original relation has been fundamentally altered and human perception is largely devoid of the former resonances of meaning that were once pervasive: "the great Pan is dead," as Plutarch so memorably proclaimed in *The Obsolescence of the Oracles*.[31] Today, poetry, properly so-called, can only issue from a creative endeavor on behalf of one with sufficient sensitivity and attunement to nature's being to perform the action reciprocal to ancient inspiration: today, the poet must give back the water of meaning to nature that his predecessors once drew from her well. *Inspiration*—that mysterious process by which the poet is supposed to have become a mouthpiece of the gods—has slowly ceased; the gods, it seems, have grown silent. Again in Plutarch's words, "the oracles have now failed completely, even as if they were streams of flowing water, and a great drought in prophecy has overspread the land."[32] But the failure of inspiration is not the end of poetry. Instead, out of the tomb of inspiration, the poet may rise again—his poetry no longer inspired from without, but kindled from within. As we shall see, this transition from inspiration to imagination is analogous to the transition from "original participation" to "final participation." Thus, in Barfield's words, "Original participation fires the heart from a source outside itself; the images enliven the heart. But in final participation—since the death and resurrection—the heart is fired from within by the Christ and it is for the heart to enliven the images."[33] Likewise, the genesis of poetry has undergone a reversal so that the function once fulfilled by inspiration is now, or at least can be, performed through imagination. The next chapters will attempt to flesh out this evolution more directly.

31. Plutarch, "De Defectu Oraculorum," Moralia, 403.

32. Plutarch, "De Defectu Oraculorum," Moralia, 363.

33. Barfield, *Saving the Appearances*, 172. See also "Philology and the Incarnation," in Barfield, *Rediscovery of Meaning*, to understand Christ's relevance to the transition from one stage to another.

4

The Evolution of
Consciousness

As with his investigation into the historical development of language, Barfield's investigation into the nature of poetry compelled him to question much that he himself, together with many of his predecessors and the majority of his contemporaries, had taken for granted about the history of the human mind and its relation to the material world. Since Barfield was unwilling to settle for a schizoid and incoherent philosophy—a philosophy that allowed conclusions in one field to be ignored from the perspective of the next—he was obliged continually to strive for a more integrated and harmonious vision among all of his spiritual and intellectual pursuits. Either the conclusions he had reached were true and needed, therefore, to be integrated into a consistent worldview or they were untrue, and therefore should not be retained at all but rather summarily rejected. Having arrived at his own philological conclusions by dint of conscientious study and reflection, Barfield perceived no reason to abandon them merely because they failed to affirm the reigning scientific paradigm of his age. Instead, Barfield set about to discover how the reigning scientific paradigm would need to be altered in order to accommodate those historical facts that seemed necessarily to be true. The fruits of this effort can be summed up by the statement that human consciousness is not a static function; it is, instead, dynamic and metamorphic, and its configuration has transformed over the course of history. As we shall see, this transformation of consciousness entails at once a transformation of the human mind as well as a transformation of the world itself in ways that cannot be accounted for by natural historians due to the self-imposed limits of their discipline. Put another way, the metamorphoses in language that Barfield first observed were revealed, on further inquiry, to reflect a transformation in the minds of the people who used that language. Given that those minds are part and parcel of the world, and must have shared a common origin out of which they both emerged, both of these terms can be expected to change together or not at all. Language represents a concrete expression of the relation between mind and world, each of which is defined in terms of the other. Hence, the evolution of language, directly observed, points to an evolution of consciousness and, *ipso facto*, of the world itself. This theory, which Barfield spent most of his life elaborating, will be the subject of this chapter and the next.

"The evolution of consciousness" is easily said but is perhaps understood only with great difficulty. As a *theory*, it is intended to do more than explain what can be readily observed. Instead, the function of a theory is more elementary than this: to wit, a theory is intended to disclose specific phenomena, patterns, and relations that may otherwise escape notice. Put another way, the function of a theory is to reveal the logic and lawfulness in what would, to the untutored eye, appear mere happenstance. Indeed, therefore, it is only in light of the proper theory that anything can be perceived, to begin with, which may then be subsequently explained. By the same token, those phenomena for which we lack a theoretical basis to conceive must also remain imperceptible to us until such time as we can elaborate such a basis. Hence, it should be clear that a theory must serve a far more fundamental function than merely providing an explanation of phenomena that have already been observed since the theory was also present as a necessary condition for any observation as such to occur. Since the meaning of the term "theory" has contracted over the last several centuries in a manner that distinctly corroborates Barfield's theory of the evolution of language, it will be necessary to recover an older, broader understanding of the term. Such an understanding will serve to better convey Barfield's argument in respect to the evolution of consciousness and to illuminate, in a more comprehensive manner, the evidence at hand that is intended to substantiate it.

Learned persons are often heard drawing a distinction between the vulgar use of *theory* as "a guess," and the scientist's technical use of the term to designate a hypothesis that has some evidential support and has survived some unspecified number of attempts at falsification. This distinction, though incomplete and somewhat facile, nevertheless serves as a helpful entry point into a more robust understanding of the term, for it highlights the fundamentally different relation that each of the meanings above bears to *evidence*. The word "evidence" combines the Latin prefix *ex-*, which is "out of" or "from," with the stem *video*, which is "I see" and which has been naturalized into English in the words "vision" and "video." Interestingly, the Latin *video* or *videre* shares an etymological relation with the *wis-* in the Saxon word "wisdom" was well as the Greek word *eidos* (εἶδος) or *idea* (ἰδέα), which are the masculine and feminine forms, respectively, of a single term which is essentially synonymous with "theory."[1] *Evidence*, then, indicates the locus or medium "out of" or "by which" something is "seen." As we will see, the *theory* or *idea* is both the means and the end of this seeing.

Returning to the two designations of theory indicated above, in the first instance (i.e., theory as guess), the relation between *theory* and *evidence* is not to be found because the theory is advanced irrespective of evidence. In the second (i.e., theory as exalted hypothesis), the relation between theory and evidence is present, despite being abstract. This is to say that it is possible to make a guess in the absence of evidence but it is, strictly speaking, not possible to assert with any credibility that a theory is valid in such conditions. A theory without evidence is not a *theory* but a *hypothesis*. And this is precisely why a distinction between these two terms should be recognized and maintained. As noted above, the union of theory and evidence, though present, is abstract in the scientific usage of this term in that the theory is often imagined as a sort of container into which evidence can be subsequently poured or laden. At the same time, people often imagine that other evidence could be gathered and subsequently laden into the theory in the same way. Hence, a theory bears only a circumstantial relation to any given datum of evidence; both the theory and the evidence are conceived abstractly and hence imagined to subsist independently of one another.

But this largely conventional view of the relation between theory and evidence subtly falls prey to the empiricist conceit alluded to in a previous chapter in the discussion of Locke's views on epistemology and the origin of language. The insufficiency of the nominalist account of perception and

---

1. The extroverted, inquisitive, and iconographic soul of the ancient Greeks is on display in their plethora of terms related to sight, just as Sanskrit demonstrates the introversion of the Indian spiritual heritage with its possession of multitudinous terms for "mind" and English hints at both its geography as well as the naturalistic, empirical disposition that is native to its speakers in, for instance, its dozens of designations for bodies of water of varying sizes. Consider, for instance: sea, lake, loch, pool, puddle, stream, brook, rivulet, ocean, mar, lagoon, river, pond, freshet, rill, channel, watercourse, runlet, waterway, fluvium, flow, flood, cascade, cataract, estuary, delta, tributary, bourn, canal, inlet, reservoir, lough, mere, and so on.

language to which Locke subscribed can here be demonstrated, for to propose that perceptible phenomena are simply lying around waiting to be labeled with nominal designations overlooks the prior cognitive activity that disclosed those objects to perception to begin with. Language is, in an essential sense, the externalization of such acts of consciousness. The intentionality of such acts is ordinarily directed to sensory phenomena but nothing is to say that it cannot be directed to non-sensory phenomena. Indeed, the word "theory" is intended to direct attention to such acts of consciousness, which are not perceptible to the physical senses but which are nevertheless perceptible and real. Indeed, as Plato famously argued some twenty-five centuries ago, these non-sensory phenomena that the mind enacts as a condition for all perception are arguably more real than any of the products of this enactment. This can be grasped by anyone capable of understanding the way in which the ideal geometrical triangle (i.e., the definition of triangle as a polygon with three vertices the sum of whose interior angles reaches exactly 180°)—a non-sensory phenomenon—is more real as a triangle than any one of its sensory or material instantiations. According to apocryphal accounts, the phrase "Let no one ignorant of geometry enter under this roof" was etched into a sign that hung over the entryway to Plato's Academy. To fructify this Platonic maxim with Barfield's insights, the diachronic corollary may be added: "Let no one ignorant in etymology embark on this journey."

It may now be seen that the question of language and perception and that of theory and evidence are hardly separate questions at all. Instead, they both demand, to be answered, an attentiveness to the cognitive activity that is the condition for any and all perception. In the face of any phenomena, whether quotidian or scientific, the fundamental axiom still holds that it is only in light of a theory that evidence of it can be recognized as such. Inversely, without a theory to disclose its relevance, evidence of it is indiscernible from mere data, of which there is a virtually infinite amount. After all, there is, in principle, no limit to the number of measurements or observations that could be performed in respect to any given phenomenon or object but no additional observation promises to deliver any insight to the perceiver unless it can be integrated, theoretically, into the meaningful context of the phenomenon in question—until this point, no "signal" is discernible from mere "noise." Hence, evidence is always a function of an idea or theory that it can be evidence for. The terms are correlative.

For this reason, it is helpful to distinguish another understanding of theory more comprehensive than the two that have hitherto been provided, one which does not abstract the means of vision from its end or object. To grasp the manner in which theory continually embodies itself, as it were, within every object of perception is to discover a concrete and integral relation between theory and evidence that intensifies the meaning of the term in question beyond the manner in which it is typically employed, even in scientific contexts. Whereas in the second instance outlined above, it is imagined that evidence is simply discovered irrespective of any theory and subsequently loaded into it, in the concrete understanding of the term, all evidence is "theory-laden" from the outset as a condition for any phenomenon to be perceived at all, and the theory could no more be removed from the evidence than a leopard could be removed from its spots. Indeed, the "theory-ladenness" of evidence was a primary concern for philosophers of science in the latter half of the twentieth century like Thomas Kuhn and Paul Feyerabend, who contributed a great deal toward advancing a more sophisticated understanding of the scientific method than had obtained to that point, and their work serves to corroborate much that Barfield said.

To follow the transformations of the meaning of theory outlined above—from "conjecture" to "hypothesis with evidential support" to "means and end of seeing"—is, in a sense, to retrace, in reverse order, an etymological evolution that has transpired over the course of millennia. The first designation above was the last to arrive in time. The common contemporary notion of theory is a derivative of its scientific usage, which in turn developed from the post-Nominalist notion of theory as an idea in the subjective mind. Originally, however, the English word "theory" meant "to see." The English term was borrowed from the Greek word *theoria* (θεωρία, *thea* "a view, a sight" + *horan* "to see"). The Latin translation of *theoria* hints at the original power of the Greek word, since the term is not translated as *coniectura, sententia,* or *hypothesi,* but as *contemplatio,* from which we derive our English word "contemplation." *Theoria* is the union of the seen with the act of seeing. That *Theos* (θεός) also means "God" in Greek, and that the Latin *contemplatio* shares the root of "temple," together hint at the numinous quality that premodern people would have experienced in the term *theoria.* The evolution of the Greek word *idea* (ιδέα)[2] follows a similar trajectory, from Plato's conception of the Ideas, sometimes rendered in the Latinate term "Forms," as the transcendent principles of the cosmos, to Aristotle's conception of ideas as the immanent actualizing principles of reality, to Aquinas's conception of ideas as the *formæ* or *species intelligibilis* of entities, to the modern conception of an idea as a merely subjective notion. A quote from Francis Bacon's *The Advancement of Learning,* a seminal work that would become something of a keynote for the nascent tradition of

---

2. *Idea* is the grammatically feminine form of *eidos* (εἶδος). Though Plato and Aristotle employed both forms, the latter appears more commonly throughout their *corpora* of work.

modern empirical science, enunciates this concept of "idea" in no uncertain terms. Bacon uses the Latin translation of the Greek word in its plural form and hence he does not speak of "Ideas" but of "Forms." The basic outlook, however, is unequivocal: "Matter rather than Forms should be the object of our attention . . . for Forms are figments of the human mind."[3]

Taken alone, the above description of these words' development may or may not interest the reader. But taken in a wider context, the concrete history of the terms "theory" and "idea," as it has been deposited in a diverse etymological strata, testifies, in the manner of a fossil record, to a history of ideas in which these terms took part. And this history of ideas—and now follows the crux of Barfield's theory—testifies, in turn, to an evolution in consciousness. It is precisely when contemplated in light of the proper theory that this evolution of consciousness *videri ex,* or "shows forth out of," the available historical evidence. Next it will be our task to elucidate some of Barfield's terminology to render this theory in sharper relief.

In *Saving the Appearances,* Barfield designates three modes of consciousness that together form a continuous spectrum, and serve as a road map of sorts, helping to orient us in our attempt to traverse the immaterial territory of any such study. These modes of consciousness can be understood in terms of degree and kind of *participation.* Indeed, the terms "mode of consciousness" and "degree and kind of participation" are, for all intents and purposes, synonymous. In other words, the evolution of consciousness and the fading of participation are coupled, like the volume and the surface area of a sphere—as one progresses, so does the other. Naturally, to begin with, it is likely no more helpful to equate these designations than it would be to explain an unfamiliar word in one's native language by providing a definition for it in a foreign tongue. For this reason, an explication of the term "participation" can be expected to aid us in our attempts to understand the evolution of consciousness. Indeed, this seems to be the map that Barfield himself laid out in *Saving the Appearances,* given that roughly a third of the book elapses before the phrase "evolution of consciousness" first appears, while the first part of the book is almost entirely concerned with characterizing different stages of participation.

As indicated, Barfield was laying the groundwork for the argument he would later advance in *Saving the Appearances* already in his early works. A shining example of this preparation appears in *History in English Words,* when Barfield describes the manner in which numerous thinkers over the

3. Bacon, *Advancement of Learning.*

last millennia, beginning with Plato, have collaborated to forge our familiar concept of *love*. Over history, each of these thinkers contributed, as it were, their stones to this temple, which transcends the particular vagaries of any one language:

> Thus, it was not only Greek words of which [Plato] was to alter the meanings, nor only Greek and Latin words. Love and good, for instance, are neither Greek nor Latin, and beauty is only Latin remotely, yet the spirit of Plato really works more amply in them, and in a hundred others bearing on the presence or absence of these qualities, than it does in such specifically Platonic terms as idea and dialectic. Let us try and trace the origin of some of the meanings which are commonly attached to the word love . . . Plato and Socrates evolved that other great conception—perhaps even more far-reaching in its historical effects—that love for a sensual and temporal object is capable of gradual metamorphosis into love for the invisible and eternal. It is not only in the New Testament and the Prayer Book, in the Divine Comedy, Shakespeare's Sonnets, and all great Romantic poetry that the results of this thinking are to be seen.[4]

In our time, it can be seen that Barfield's work played a comparable role to what Plato achieved in respect to the concept of *love* in respect to the

4. Full passage: "Thus, it was not only Greek words of which [Plato] was to alter the meanings, nor only Greek and Latin words. Love and good, for instance, are neither Greek nor Latin, and beauty is only Latin remotely, yet the spirit of Plato really works more amply in them, and in a hundred others bearing on the presence or absence of these qualities, than it does in such specifically Platonic terms as idea and dialectic. Let us try and trace the origin of some of the meanings which are commonly attached to the word love. As in the Mysteries, so at the heart of early Greek philosophy lay two fundamental assumptions. One was that an inner meaning lay hid behind external phenomena. Out of this Plato's lucid mind brought to the surface of Europe's consciousness the stupendous conception that all matter is but an imperfect copy of spiritual 'types' or 'ideas'—eternal principles which, so far from being abstractions, are the only real Beings, which were in their place before matter came into existence, and which will remain after it has passed away. The other assumption concerned the attainment by man of immortality. The two were complementary. Just as it was only the immortal part of man which could get into touch with the eternal secret behind the changing forms of Nature, so also it was only by striving to contemplate that eternal that man could develop the eternal part of himself and put on incorruption. There remained the question of how to rise from the contemplation of the transient to the contemplation of the eternal, and, for answer, Plato and Socrates evolved that other great conception—perhaps even more far-reaching in its historical effects—that love for a sensual and temporal object is capable of gradual metamorphosis into love for the invisible and eternal. It is not only in the New Testament and the Prayer Book, in the Divine Comedy, Shakespeare's Sonnets, and all great Romantic poetry that the results of this thinking are to be seen." Barfield, *History in English Words*, 106–7.

concept of *participation.* The latter is not an idea that is original to Barfield. At the same time, it will be evident that it is an idea that he imbued with new dimensions of significance through his labors. Indeed, it is precisely Barfield's energetic engagement with the subject already in his university years, as evinced through the later publication of his undergraduate thesis under the title of *Poetic Diction,* that allowed him, half a century later, to offer, in his monograph of Coleridge's philosophy, such a concise definition of participation as "the felt union with the inner origin of outward forms."[5]

Far from emerging fully armed from the young thinker's head, the idea of participation, as indicated above, traces deep roots in the history of philosophy. For instance, participation was a technical term for the School-men of the Middle Ages. These philosophers, in turn, inherited it together with that aureate trove of philosophy that we recognize under the rubric of "the Classics." Plato, Aristotle, the New Testament and Neo-Platonist writers like Paul, Plotinus, Proclus, Boethius, and Dionysius the Areopagite each contributed in his own way toward enriching the concept. Obviously, these philosophers did not write in English and hence they did not employ the term "participation." Instead, they expressed this notion with terms like *metalepsis* (μετάληψις), *methexis* (μέθεξις), or sometimes *koinonia* (κοινωνία). Each of these terms indicates a "taking part in," and gestures towards a union or synergy that nevertheless preserves the individuality of its members. Barfield quotes Aquinas's characteristically lucid explanation of the term from the preface to the latter's commentary on Boethius's *De hebdomadibus.* Here Aquinas distinguishes three genera of participation:

1. A *particular* takes part in, which is to say, participates, a *universal.* He offers the following examples of this genus of participation: man participates animal, and Socrates participates man. This can be under-stood according to the logical principle of entailment: a part of a part is a part of the whole.

2. Similarly, a *subject* participates its *accident* just as *matter* participates *form.* Aquinas did not feel it necessary to offer any examples of this second genus, but we could borrow an idiosyncratic example from Aristotle and say that Socrates participates "snub-nosedness" because he, as a subject, apparently possessed a snub nose, as an accident. Simi-larly, blood and bones participate Socrates as a physical being because Socrates is the *form* of blood and bones, and the latter, in turn, are the

5. Barfield, *What Coleridge Thought,* 160.

matter of their respective *form*, which is Socrates.[6] These are examples
of subject-accident and matter-form relations, respectively.

3. Also, an effect participates its cause. Barfield specifically cites the example that Aquinas offers in this case: "Suppose we say that air participates the light of the sun, because it does not receive it in that clarity
in which it is in the sun."[7] The sun being the cause of the light, the air
participates that cause.

In sum, every particular participates its correlative universal, all matter participates its correlative form, every effect participates its correlative cause,
and so on. Taken further, the cosmos can be understood as the participation
of all beings in Being: *plura entia, sed non plus entis,* which is, "many beings
but not more Being." Indeed, the consummation of the philosophic ascent
can be understood as an intellectual apprehension of Creation *as* participation, in which every creature takes part in its own transcendence. The vision of catholic participation in the Good-beyond-Being is the same thing
as theophany. Precisely this participatory structure of Creation establishes
a sort of spiritual recursivity such that the noetic structure of the cosmos
that is revealed upon the loftiest spiritual ascent can be recognized at any

---

6. Cf. Plato's *Phaedo* dialogue: "As I proceeded, I found my philosopher altogether
forsaking mind or any other principle of order, but having recourse to air, and ether,
and water, and other eccentricities. I might compare him to a person who began by
maintaining generally that mind is the cause of the actions of Socrates, but who, when
he endeavoured to explain the causes of my several actions in detail, went on to show
that I sit here because my body is made up of bones and muscles; and the bones, as
he would say, are hard and have joints which divide them, and the muscles are elastic,
and they cover the bones, which have also a covering or environment of flesh and skin
which contains them; and as the bones are lifted at their joints by the contraction or
relaxation of the muscles, I am able to bend my limbs, and this is why I am sitting here
in a curved posture—that is what he would say, and he would have a similar explanation of my talking to you, which he would attribute to sound, and air, and hearing, and
he would assign ten thousand other causes of the same sort, forgetting to mention the
true cause, which is, that the Athenians have thought fit to condemn me, and accordingly I have thought it better and more right to remain here and undergo my sentence;
for I am inclined to think that these muscles and bones of mine would have gone off
long ago to Megara or Boeotia—by the dog they would, if they had been moved only
by their own idea of what was best, and if I had not chosen the better and nobler part,
instead of playing truant and running away, of enduring any punishment which the
state inflicts. There is surely a strange confusion of causes and conditions in all this. It
may be said, indeed, that without bones and muscles and the other parts of the body I
cannot execute my purposes. But to say that I do as I do because of them, and that this
is the way in which mind acts, and not from the choice of the best, is a very careless and
idle mode of speaking. I wonder that they cannot distinguish the cause from the condition, which the many, feeling about in the dark, are always mistaking and misnaming."

7. Barfield, *Saving the Appearances*, 90.

scale—"a World in a Grain of Sand" and "Eternity in an hour," as Blake so memorably made the point.

The concept of participation has been further enriched in modern times by anthropologists. Barfield begins his own exposition of the nature of participation in *Saving the Appearances* by appealing to the theories of Lucien Lévy-Bruhl, who posited that primitive people subsisted in a state of *participation mystique,* or "psychic participation" with everything in their environment.[8] Put another way, the experience of another being was also, in part, an identification with that being. In the words of Carl Jung, who made use of Lévy-Bruhl's idea in the development of his own psychological theory, "[*participation mystique*] denotes a peculiar kind of psychological connection with objects, and consists in the fact that the subject cannot clearly distinguish himself from the object but is bound to it by a direct relationship which amounts to partial identity."[9] To imaginatively enter into this condition has the power to cast Bishop Berkeley's doctrine of *esse est percipi*—ordinarily construed as a keynote of subjective idealism—in an entirely different light. Perhaps it could be read at the same time as *percipere esse est:* "to perceive is also to be." In any case, Barfield corroborates Lévy-Bruhl's view by relating it to his own theory in respect to the evolution of language.

We may recall from prior chapters that language begins in a condition of semantic unity and subsequently stretches into the future through a process of fracture and ramification. In establishing this connection between philology and anthropology, Barfield also succeeds in situating Lévy-Bruhl's theories in an evolutionary context. In other words, Barfield demonstrates how the *participation mystique* was not simply an ancient condition that *happened* to obtain amongst primitive peoples and which was later replaced by a different condition. Instead, by indexing *participation mystique* to the same spectrum of development that Barfield himself had identified in the transformation of language, Barfield succeeded in revealing the inner logic of this change. As a result, it no longer appeared as a mere item of historical trivia that primitive man sustained an entirely different relationship with his surroundings from the one that we do today. On the contrary, this single datum represents evidence of the most profound philosophical significance to those with eyes to see *through*, and a theory to see *with*.

The connection of Barfield's work to Lévy-Bruhl's also serves to flesh out the essential subject that is undergoing this development to begin with. The subject is, of course, the human being and the pattern of its development naturally finds expression in both anthropological and philological

8. See chapter 4 of *Saving the Appearances.*
9. Jung, *Psychological Types*, 456.

contexts. A single sense might register warmth and another brightness, but without the common sense, which is to say the mind or soul,[10] these percepts would remain discrete and the single flame that is their shared source would fail to be apprehended. In a similar way, it might have been that Levy-Bruhl's work would have remained separated off from Barfield's in a "water-tight compartment"[11] and no relation between the *participation mystique* and the evolution of language would have been recognized. When it is grasped, however, that these two phenomena are in fact expressions of the same phenomenon, our insight into the significance of each of them is infinitely deepened, just as warmth and brightness attain a new dimension of meaning when they are apprehended as two aspects of a single flame.

Barfield argues that humanity's experience of participation appeared to diminish in the course of history. Beginning from the *participation mystique,* which Barfield calls "Original Participation," individual consciousness increasingly appears to condense out of a common field. One might imagine the precipitation of salt crystals from a saline solution as an analogy for the manner in which mind at large—the cosmic *nous* of the ancient Greek thinkers—was increasingly concentrated in individual brains. Barfield even writes of a "sinewy quality in Aristotle's νους ποιητικός νους παθετικος (*nous poieticus* and *nous patheticus*), which has already faded somewhat from their Latin equivalents *intellectus agens* and *intellectus possibilis*."[12] He concludes that the "*nous* of which Aristotle spoke and thought was clearly less subjective than Aquinas's *intellectus*."[13] Hence, it can be observed that consciousness undergoes a sort of inwardization or individuation in the course of history. Remarkably, this transformation can be grasped both *phylogenetically* and *ontogenetically*.

In the first instance, we may consider the manner in which life is conjectured to have emerged out of nonliving elements. A full-scale acceptance of theoretical abiogenesis is unnecessary to invoke the imaginal sequence of life incorporating and arraying itself in the matter of physical elements. It will be seen that life could not take *actual* manifestation except in the presence of *potential* for it to become so manifest. Hence, even in a hypothetical state of the cosmos in which no life was yet present, it nevertheless remains clear that that same cosmos must necessarily have been of such a nature as to contain life in potency if not yet in actuality, for "nothing will come

---

10. I.e., Latin *sensus communis*, Greek αἴσθησις κοινὴ, *aísthēsis koinè̄*, which Aristotle described as the synthesizing power of the animate soul to join the percepts provided by the divers senses into a coherent perception.

11. Cf. Barfield, *Worlds Apart*.

12. Barfield, *Saving the Appearances*, 100.

13. Barfield, *Saving the Appearances*, 100.

of nothing."[14] And the actual manifestation of life consists precisely in life embodying or enfolding itself in matter in the manner indicated above. Put another way, life emerges as *actuality* in nature in direct proportion to its having been siphoned off and appropriated from the life at large that subsists in a state of cosmic *potentiality*. Similarly, the emergence of sentience and locomotion must have consisted in just such a manner of appropriation in which individual beings drew upon a cosmic potentiality of sentience and will. Again, neither sentience nor locomotion could have evolved in a universe that was devoid of the possibility for such an evolution. By the same token, the fact that these phenomena did indeed evolve evinces something specific about the nature of the present universe, which is the only one there is. Once the pattern of actualization through inwardization is grasped through its instances in the evolution of life and sentience, it can be discovered again in the process by which humanity began to individuate the cosmic *logos*, the *nous*, the *intellectus*, from out of its transcendent potentiality. This graduated inwardization of mind was experienced as the protracted dawning of self-awareness. Until the *logos* has been taken in and individuated, it is impossible for a being to say "I." After this time, it becomes increasingly difficult not to.[15] Barfield explains how the comparatively recent individuation of selfhood can be so easily overlooked:

> The consciousness of "myself" and the distinction between "myself" and all other selves . . . is such an obvious and early fact of experience to every one of us . . . that it really requires a sort of training of the imagination to be able to conceive of any different kind of consciousness. Yet we can see from the history of our words that this form of experience, so far from being eternal, is quite a recent achievement of the human spirit.[16]

The coalescence of selfhood can thus be understood as a specific event in the course of world history. In the manner that visible light is conceived to occupy a definite though narrow band on the entire electromagnetic spectrum, so the transformations in participation that Barfield outlined can be understood to occupy particular moments in the cosmic evolution of life and mind.

14. Cf. Shakespeare, *King Lear*, I.1.

15. Jung saw the same implication from the fading of *participation mystique*: "The further we go back into history, the more we see personality disappearing beneath the wrappings of collectivity. And if we go right back to primitive psychology, we find absolutely no trace of the concept of an individual. Instead of individuality we find only collective relationship or what Lévy-Bruhl calls *participation mystique*." *Psychological Types*, 10.

16. Barfield, *History in English Words*, 169.

Here a brief excursus is perhaps in order into the word *psyche*. Such an exploration will at once serve to illuminate the topic at hand as well as to provide yet another concrete demonstration of an anterior semantic unity ramifying into discrete lexemes just as a wave function may decohere and collapse into local particles. The Greek word *psyche* (Ψυχή), which has been naturalized into English as a rough synonym to "soul," appears to possess a far more encompassing semantic field than any one of its potential English equivalents. This phenomenon ought at once to alert us of the likelihood that *psyche*, like *pneuma*, which we considered in chapter 2, is a word whose "heart has been torn to shreds" by the marauding aions and which must be restored by the imaginative faculty of the poet if any insight into its anterior semantic unity is to be attained.[17] In his treatise on the soul, often referred to by its Latin title of *De Anima*,[18] Aristotle had delineated several "gradients" of soul, from the "vegetative" or "nourishing" soul, which extends as far as plant life, to the "sentient" and "locomotive" soul, which "animates" animal life, to the "rational soul," which incarnates itself in man of the natural kingdom. Aristotle's terms for these gradients of soul were *to threptikon* (plant), *to aisthetikon* (sensation), *to kinetikon* (motion), and *dianoetikon* (reason), respectively. The transition between gradients is best considered as an *intensification* or an *increase* in *dimensions of inwardness*. Hence, whereas the inanimate object's form and transformations are dictated entirely by the environment in which it finds itself, the plant, possessed of the first degree of *psyche*, has inwardized the formal principles of generation and propagation into itself. Flowers tend to become seeds that tend to become new flowers. This progression happens in the context of, and to some degree, in spite of, environmental factors. After all, wind scatters dust while a plant, which may bear approximately the same proportions of physical elements, strives, against the elements, to maintain its formal integrity. In this way, the plant is influenced by external forces but it also bears an immanent directedness towards the realization of its innate potential. Hence, the plant is both shaped by, but also contributes to the shape of, its environment.

17. Of course, the allusion is to the following quote from *Poetic Diction* (28): "Science deals with the world which it perceives but, seeking more and more to penetrate the veil of naïve perception, progresses only towards the goal of nothing, because it still does not accept in practice (whatever it may admit theoretically) that the mind first creates what it perceives as objects, including the instruments which Science uses for that very penetration. It insists on dealing with 'data,' but there shall no data be given, save the bare percept. The rest is imagination. Only by imagination therefore can the world be known. And what is needed is, not only that larger and larger telescopes and more and more sensitive calipers should be constructed, but that the human mind should become increasingly aware of its own creative activity."

18. Originally titled Περί Ψυχῆς, or *Peri Psychēs*.

It will be clear from a moment's reflection that animals have inwardized further principles that set them apart from flora while, at the same time, they also take part in the principle that sets flora apart from mere matter, or life from mere physics. A moment's observation will reveal that animals exhibit a periodic pattern of spatial expansion and contraction that we recognize and designate as "respiration." This phenomenon likely accounts for another common translation of *psyche* as "breath." The plant's "respiration" is not its own and is rather a participation of the earth's seasons—a sort of "breathing in" and then releasing of sunlight through photosynthesis and then decay. Indeed, the inspiration of a plant correlates with its germinal phases and its expiration with its flowering, fruiting, and withering and/or combustion. This pattern is recapitulated in the microcosm of an animal's physiology. Aristotle identifies the distinctive elements of the animal soul as the capacities for sensation and for (loco)motion. Respiration in the animal can be thought of as a sort of inflection point between the *centripetal* impulse of sense perception and the *centrifugal* impulse of motion. This accounts for the "restless" and "labile" qualities that the animal soul imparts into the purely vegetative soul. The most phlegmatic animal is infinitely more volatile than the most restive plant. Plants fix carbon through photosynthesis while animals unfix it through respiratory combustion.

The animal's consciousness is manifestly coupled with its environment. Despite that animals clearly exhibit intentional behavior, and can therefore be presumed to experience meaningful perceptions, the meaningfulness is entirely bound to specific phenomena in the animals' surroundings. For the human being, meaning is incrementally uncoupled from specific sense-perceptions of the environment. "The world," therefore, increasingly takes on a purely sensory connotation in order to function as a theoretical matrix to organize our sensory percepts. At the same time, meanings begin to be experienced inwardly, within the capacious dimensions of the conscious or rational soul and are thereby increasingly sundered from the world outside. This polarization of sense-perception and meaning expresses itself in the emergence of language and thought. Indeed, as breath may be seen as an external manifestation of the animal soul, speech must be considered an outward sign of the rational one. At the same time, thought must be seen as an inward sign. Thus, the rational soul may be conceived as an individuated participation of the *logos* or the *nous*, which clearly represents a further intensification of *psyche* beyond its floral and animal strata. Each of these gradients of soul, from formation, to sensation, to locomotion, to self-conscious reason, appears to follow upon the ones that precede it in the manner that the blossom of flower depends on everything green that came before it. To complete the analogy, *psyche* is bounded on both ends just as a flower finds itself suspended between the earth and the sun. Entirely unappropriated psyche can be recognized as what we would likely today term "energy" or "force" in its material pole and "mind" or "intelligence" in its noetic pole. Hence, the human being can be said, on one hand, to possess his own personal intelligence, and on the other hand, to participate the cosmic intelligence.

Indeed, through the Middle Ages, Christian philosophers preserved the distinction, first designated by Plato and Aristotle, between the intellect or the *nous* and the rational soul or *dianoetikon*. The latter term indicated the function of discursive reason while the former pointed to a direct intuitive apprehension of ideas and essences. *Rationality* provides knowledge through inference while *intellection* provides knowledge through participation. These could also be termed "soul" and "spirit," respectively; the first indicating a certain function enclosed in itself and the second the same function in participation with its origin and destiny. Already with the Fourth Council of Constantinople in 869 AD, however, the distinction between the two functions of the mind was being threatened—proximately, by internecine conflicts and ultimately by the loss of Original Participation. In the proceedings from the council, Pope Hadrian II decreed, against Photios, that the human being possesses a singular rational-intellectual soul[19] alone and "let anyone who denies this fact be anathema." Hence, per the 11th Canon of the Eighth Ecumenical Council, it was no longer permitted to speak of the trichotomy of body, soul, and spirit—or body, rationality, and intellection, in terms consistent with the argument above—in respect to the constitution of the human being. Man was thus cut off from above and uncoupled from the *scala naturæ* or the "Great Chain of Being." The spiritual element of man was increasingly seen as a function of the soul alone while *psyche* itself was increasingly equated with our more familiar conception of "soul" as an approximate synonym with "personal self." The significance of the apparently abstruse dogmatic pronouncement in the 11th Canon is that intellection, which is to say, the soul's participation in objective essences of things, was increasingly construed as a purely psychic function. As a result, intellection was increasingly equated with mere rationicination; the *nous* ceased to be distinguished from the *dianoetikon*.

By the early modern period, the soul was imagined as entirely self-contained and hence incapable of participation in anything outside of itself. Whereas the Eighth Ecumenical Council had severed the soul's connection to the spirit, the soul's identity with the body was affirmed with increasing univocality to the point that a contemporary scientist can, without a second

---

19. "*Unam animam rationabilem et intellectualem.*"

thought, equate the activity of the mind with the physiology of the brain. Of course, countercurrents to the materialist trend have always existed. Thus, Goethe, in the eighteenth century, could speak of a capacity of *Aunschaunde Urteilskraft,* or "intellectual intuition"[20] through which it was possible to enter into "a spiritual participation . . . in the productions of an ever-creating Nature."[21] Indeed, Goethe, Schelling, and the other German Idealists, distinguished between *der Verstand,* on one hand, which corresponded to the Latin *ratio,* and *die Vernunft,* which corresponded to the Latin *intellectus.* Regrettably, English translations often obscured the distinction following the unfortunate translation of *Vernunft* as "Reason" and *Verstand* as "intellect" or "understanding." Note that, as a consequence, "intellect" now refers to a function that the Scholastics knew as *ratio,* which they set in contradistinction to the *intellectus.* The result of this reversal is that we almost never really know what we are talking about in English when the question broaches these capacities of mind and soul. Still, the logic behind the confusion of terms is evident in light of the evolution of consciousness. To wit, the loss of experienced participation entails the loss of the ability to directly participate the archetypal ideas. Thus, even with vocabulary to establish this distinction with clarity, the ascendant state of general consciousness does not allow for the words to continue to mean what they once had. Thus, Goethe's intellectual intuition into the morphology of plants were largely dismissed as pseudoscience by his German contemporaries.[22]

Following this excursus into the meaning and historical metamorphosis of the term *psyche,* we may return to the vision of its involution by degrees as expressed in phylogenetic lines of descent, which establishes the context and paradigm to situate the evolution of consciousness. First, however, we may observe that a grasp of the concept of "soul" such as that which an ancient Greek thinker would have possessed will only be attained by a

20. Roughly, "the power of intellective judgment." Cf. Part 2 of Treinen, *Redemption of Thinking* for a more thorough treatment of this topic.

21. Cf. Goethe: "If, then, in a moral sense, we are, through faith in God, to attain to youth and immortality in a higher region, and are to draw near to the Most High, it should surely be the same in an intellectual sense, that only by the contemplation of an ever-creating Nature, we shall become worthy of spiritual participation in her productions." Quoted from an address given by Rudolf Steiner, "Spiritual-Scientific Basis of Goethe's Work."

22. Little did it likely occur to the latter that their dismissal was largely predicated less on necessary limits to cognition than on the unconscious basis of upholding a dogmatic decree from the ninth century, whose power and historical persistence derived from its conformity with the basic trend in the evolution of consciousness.

contemporary English speaker with great difficulty. To the ancient Greek, *psyche* was bounded by the poles of physics from below and pure *nous* from above, and spanned the entire range in between. Thus, either "soul" may come to mean much more than we think today or it is not an adequate translation of *psyche*. To understand the concrete meaning of *psyche*, it is evident that we must conceive of a word that means neither "life," nor "sentience," nor "animation," nor "fire," nor "light," nor "breath," nor "mind," nor "spirit," but all of these at once. The human being, which is to say, "the bearer of mind,"[23] ostensibly the latest to arrive, finds itself possessed of the greatest dimensions of *psyche* so as to summarize all prior kingdoms—"So the last shall be first, and the first last," as it were.[24] Indeed, man has traditionally been considered as something of a compendium of the natural world; a microcosm that displays a stamp of the entire universe.[25] In Barfield's words:

> Before the scientific revolution, [man] did not feel himself isolated by his skin from the world outside to quite the same extent that we do. He was integrated, or mortised into it, each different part of him being united to a different part of it by some invisible thread. In his relation to his environment, the man of the middle ages was rather less like an island, rather more like an embryo.

In the spirit of Haeckle's so-called "biogenetic law"—to wit, that "ontogeny recapitulates phylogeny"[26]—it can be seen how every individual rehearses the entire process of evolution in miniature in his or her own biography. The same pattern operative in the descent of man may be discovered again in the genesis of every human. From here it can be seen again how the individual participates in the principle of the species both as a member of the greater

23. The etymology of human is somewhat murky but it is likely a combination of *hum-*, as in "humus," which stems from the Proto-Indo-European root *dhghem*, which is "earth," and *man*, which stems from the Proto-Indo-European word for "mind." Compare to Sanskrit *manas* and Latin *mens*. Hence, "human" leaves one with the image of a union of spirit and matter or heaven and earth, the incorporation of mind in the dust of the earth.

24. Matthew 20:16.

25 Barfield, *Saving the Appearances*, 78.

26. Cf. Haeckel, *Riddle of the Universe at the Close of the Nineteenth Century:* "I established the opposite view, that this history of the embryo (ontogeny) must be completed by a second, equally valuable, and closely connected branch of thought—the history of race (phylogeny). Both of these branches of evolutionary science are, in my opinion, in the closest causal connection; this arises from the reciprocal action of the laws of heredity and adaptation . . . 'ontogenesis is a brief and rapid recapitulation of phylogenesis, determined by the physiological functions of heredity (generation) and adaptation (maintenance).'"

pattern as well as a fractal instantiation of it. In this way, it is possible to discern the manner in which the intelligible history of humanity advances a cosmic archetype. As plant life advanced this pattern of involution by taking in the first degree of soul, and animal life added to it by enfolding the second and third ones, so man enfolds a further dimension of inwardness by taking into himself the *logos*, which is to say, the principle of meaning. Moreover, it can be seen how the entire process is both summed up by, and carried forward in, the life of each and every individual. What soil is to the plant, the soul is to the *logos*.

It is crucial to note at this point the somewhat paradoxical nature of the particular dimension of inwardness that humankind is currently enfolding. Namely, humanity's participation in this particular stage in the cosmic process has resulted in a loss of the consciousness of participation in that very process. The so-called "descent of man"[27] describes a gradual departure from the state of Original Participation to one in which human beings experience themselves as atomic individuals entirely cut off from the cosmic process itself. Barfield, borrowing a phrase from the work of Ernst Lehrs, describes this condition as "Onlooker Consciousness."[28] This state is perhaps most iconically depicted in the proverbial Cartesian subject who peers out at the world of *res extensa* through the keyholes of his senses but remains, as a *res cogitans* entirely ensconced within his cranium.[29] But the loss of the experience of participation is not the same thing as the loss of participation *per se* anymore than the Sirens' song ceased to sound when Odysseus shut his ears to it. And indeed, Barfield's vision of the evolution of consciousness can only be fully understood through a perception of its axial symmetry. Because we find ourselves concretely set in the midst of a process and not at its completion, this symmetry only reveals itself to the eye of the imagination and not to sense. The *actual* descent of man, to be understood, must be grasped in the context of the *potential* for re-ascent that that same descent engenders. Cartesian dualism articulates Jonah's view from the belly of the whale. Indeed, it is precisely the concentration of consciousness into the individual that at once severs that individual from an awareness of his

27. Cf. the title of Charles Darwin's 1871 work in which he applied evolutionary theory the human being.

28. Ernst Lehrs, *Man or Matter*. Lehrs, like Barfield was influenced by Coleridge who, despite being fascinated with Newton, criticized his system of thought for assuming that the mind "is always passive—a lazy onlooker on an external world."

29. Strictly speaking, this makes no sense since it is precisely a lack of spatial extension that defines *res cogitans*. Hence, it cannot really be said to be any*where*. Descartes seems never to have troubled himself much by this paradox, as evinced by the fact that he considered "the pineal gland" to be a satisfactory solution to the riddle of how the material body interfaces with the immaterial soul. Cf. Descartes, *Passions of the Soul*.

continuity with all of creation and also provides the possibility for reunion in full self-consciousness. Indeed, such concentration of consciousness into individual loci—conceived nonspatially[30]—serves to establish the intensification of that same consciousness that is necessary if it is to reintegrate itself, with intention, individuality, and lucidity, into a participation in the cosmic whole. It bears emphasis that in accomplishing this reintegration, the human being is not merely returning to a prior state. To do so would represent no great achievement and would certainly not have warranted the intellectual and spiritual labor that Barfield and others[31] have put into elaborating this theory. Indeed, any time a person sleeps or drinks opium, he or she essentially reenters into the state of Original Participation. But that is to insist on returning empty-handed to the table of the gods; to force one's way into the wedding feast with neither a gift nor a proper vestment. Instead, the return from the exile of Onlooker Consciousness is accomplished only after having won a pearl of great price: namely, individuality, or self-consciousness. Barfield's term for this future state is "Final Participation."

To grasp the nature of Final Participation, it will perhaps be helpful to review several further designations that Barfield lays out in *Saving the Appearances*. "Look at a rainbow," Barfield enjoins his reader in the first sentence of the work. He goes on to make the apparently trivial observation that the rainbow is a phenomenon. But, like so many of Barfield's insights, its profundity is liable to escape the distracted reader. To be a phenomenon means to be perceived. Again, one may be reminded of Berkeley's axiom, which is ordinarily discounted as an extremist stance. But *phenomena*, by definition, must be conceived in precisely the way that Berkeley's axiom indicates since *phenomenon* literally means "appearance" or "representation."[32] Hence it makes as little sense to speak of an unperceived or unrepresented phenomenon as to speak of a shapeless hexagon. Barfield observes that, whatever else we may wish to claim about the phenomena, we must acknowledge that they do not preexist our minds' participation in their appearance. Hence, far

30. Concentration into "a self," which is not necessarily interchangeable with "a body." Otherwise we could not distinguish a living body from a corpse.

31. Perhaps most notably, Rudolf Steiner. Barfield writes of Steiner: "As to the substance of his teachings and his life, I cannot see him otherwise than as a key figure —perhaps on the human level, the key figure—in the painful transition of humanity from what I have ventured to call original participation to final participation . . . In him we observe, actually beginning to occur, the transition from *homo sapiens* to *homo imaginans et amans*." From "Introducing Rudolf Steiner."

32. From ancient Greek φαινόμενον, *phainómenon*.

from the image of the Cartesian theater in which objects utterly heterogeneous to the mind succeed, by a sort of conjuring trick, in becoming perceptions for it, Barfield offers a view in which the mind is already latent in every
object of perception. He called this function "figuration." Figuration refers,
more or less, to the process that Coleridge denoted with the term "Primary
Imagination."[33] In Barfield's description from *Saving the Appearances,*

> as the organs of sense are required to convert the unrepresented
> ("particles") into sensations for us, so something is required in
> us to convert sensations into "things." It is this something that
> I mean. And it will avoid confusion if I purposely choose an
> unfamiliar and little-used word and call it, at the risk of infelic-
> ity, *figuration.*

Far from the empiricist notion of the mind as a more or less passive onlooker to the external world, therefore, Barfield, following Coleridge and in
parallel with various schools of phenomenology, means to draw the reader's
attention to the mind's ubiquitous and continual virtuality in all perception.
Barfield has sometimes been accused of advancing a kind of "closet Kan-
tianism." Are not "the unrepresented" or "the particles" just another term
for the unknowable *noumenon* or "thing-in-itself" that Kant had posited as
existing forever beyond our ability to reach it? No, because Barfield is referring to what is not represented and not what is not representable. An unread
letter is not the same thing as an unreadable letter, even if it is written in
what, to me, may be a foreign tongue. Similarly, Barfield is not attempting
to establish limits to knowledge but to describe features of cognition and
perception that are self-evident upon reflection.

Going further, Barfield invites us to consider an alternative to the typical analogy of the mind as an empty box into which impressions and ideas
can be put, or a blank slate upon which external objects impress themselves.
Instead, Barfield suggests that the mind relates to its objects of perception
not as a *container* to its *contents* but as *virtuality* to *actuality.* In this case,
the more fitting model for the mind's relation to nature would be that which

33. In Coleridge's words: "The Imagination then I consider either as primary, or
secondary. The primary Imagination I hold to be the living Power and prime Agent of
all human Perception, and as a repetition in the finite mind of the eternal act of creation
in the infinite I Am. The secondary I consider as an echo of the former, co-existing
with the conscious will, yet still as identical with the primary in the kind of its agency,
and differing only in degree, and in the mode of its operation. It dissolves, diffuses,
dissipates, in order to re-create; or where this process is rendered impossible, yet still
at all events it struggles to idealize and to unify. It is essentially vital, even as all objects
(as objects) are essentially fixed and dead." Coleridge, *Biographia Literaria,* Ch. 13. See
Barfield's analysis of this passage in chapter 3 of *What Coleridge Thought.*

holds between the conscious mind and the unconscious one. As Barfield suggests in his monograph on Coleridge:

> It is because reason is present in nature, and not merely because of the repressed physical appetites, or of physically "inherited" memories, that we can speak fruitfully of a "consciousness, which lies *beneath* or (as it were) *behind* the spontaneous conscious-ness natural to all reflecting beings" and that it nevertheless makes sense to call this consciousness-beneath-consciousness "philosophic." Indeed, the best way of approaching the relation between reason's "presence in" nature and its "presence to" the understanding, may well be to think in terms of the uncon-scious" and consciousness." . . . What was present but asleep as life in nature becomes, when present to the understanding, the awakener.[34]

Elsewhere, Barfield elaborates on this theme by observing that the phe-nomenal world cannot coherently be thought of as "external" in a spatial sense. The external world, he writes, "is not outside of man in the sense of being independent of him, but is his outside in the sense that every inside has a correlative outside; that it is the obverse of his self-consciousness: his self-consciousness displayed before him, so to speak, as his perception."[35] Conventional wisdom holds that consciousness emerged at some point in evolution as a sort of epiphenomenon of brain processes, resulting from the conjectured survival and reproductive utility that it, *ex hypothesi,* must have conferred on our ancestors. Barfield emphatically rejects this simplistic view: a hexagon cannot be freed from its shape without being freed from existence altogether and in attempting to grasp the relation between mind and world, we are asked to conceive of a relation no less essential. The mind is not an afterthought to nature.

We will, very shortly, find an occasion to enter more deeply into this theme where we hope that any eventual objections to this proposition may receive an adequate response. First, however, let it be noted that, in spite of the hidden homogeneity of mind and world, it is nevertheless possible to treat the objects of perception *as if* they existed independently. Moreover, it may even be advisable to do this in many instances. Indeed, it is not at all difficult to make a case for the utility of assuming this specific intentional-ity toward objects of the material world on purely Darwinian grounds. In other words, *objects* of perception may be regarded as though they subsisted

34. Barfield, *What Coleridge Thought,* 130.

35. Barfield, "Participation and Isolation," in *Rediscovery of Meaning and Other Es-says,* 302.

independently of the *subjects* of those perceptions. "Alpha thinking" is the term that Barfield coins to designate this mode of thought. Alpha thinking is predicated on the belief in the supremacy of a sort of "view-from-nowhere" in which, as noted, the subject is extracted from its field of perceptual relations but the objects of these relations are retained. Indeed, alpha thinking characterizes the majority of what passes for science and philosophy since the Enlightenment and the so-called "modern period" in science and philosophy. Of course, the assumptions of postmodernism present a stark challenge to this familiar view but the former have, from the looks of things, failed to adequately distinguish between suspicion of metanarratives and suspicion of truth and reality *simplicter*. Thus, despite that the star of postmodernism may have been on the rise since the publication of *Saving the Appearances,* it remains far from midheaven and the Empirico-rationalist conceit—that atomic material entities constitute the essential elements of reality—remains the tacit consensus among the vast majority of thinkers, irrespective of how much they may affirm one or another of various fashionable alternatives. If this were not the case and the objects of perception were seen to be bound in an essential relation with their percipients, science and philosophy would display an immediate, necessary, and unremitting interest in the moral and intellectual transformation of their practitioners.[36] If anything, today there is less interest in such cultivation than at any other time in history and hence the objection that the modernist conceit is obsolete can be provisionally put to rest.

Regarding the function of alpha thinking: it was suggested that the world viewed through this mode of thought is the familiar view-from-nowhere world of natural history and the natural sciences. Many imagine that consciousness is a very late arrival on the scene in this picture and that numberless eons of stars careening in their orbits and nebulae exploding into celestial elements transpired before the first faint flickers of consciousness emerged on the stage of universal history. More significantly, many imagine that mind could be hypothetically extracted from the universe and its history, and the latter would have nevertheless played out exactly as it

36. Barfield alludes to the corollary of the integral view in *Saving the Appearances* when he writes: "We should remember this, when appraising the aberrations of the formally representational arts. Of course, in so far as these are due to affectation, they are of no importance. But in so far as they are genuine, they are genuine because the artist has in some way or other experienced the world he represents. And in so far as they are appreciated, they are appreciated by those who are themselves willing to make a move towards seeing the world in that way, and, ultimately therefore, seeing that kind of world. We should remember this, when we see pictures of a dog with six legs emerging from a vegetable marrow or a woman with a motor-bicycle substituted for her left breast." *Saving the Appearances,* 137.

is believed to have done in fact, notwithstanding the absence of this single apparently trivial detail. Alpha thinking is naturally oblivious to itself and hence prone to dismiss its own existence as an afterthought—an epiphenomenon of more fundamental processes.

But, of course, to adopt something as a methodological postulate is not to be confused with advancing a defensible assertion of that thing as fact. Indeed, serious reflection will at once reveal the impossibility that the existence of consciousness can be adequately grasped from the departure point outside of consciousness on the premise that the phenomenal world bears, to begin with, no relation to the mind that perceives it. It may be objected that the assertion of mind as an elementary feature of creation smacks of superstition and pseudoscience. But it is only possible to level this objection from the outlook of alpha thinking alone—an arrested alpha thinking at that, for on the basis of what evidence can it be posited that the world could just as well exist entirely bereft of subjectivity? After all, any inquiry into this question at all already presupposes the very thing it is attempting to disprove. But more pressingly, any evidence for this hypothesis, even in the (perhaps impossible) absence of a researcher for whom it could present as evidence, would have to be drawn from an alternative universe to our own, since the present one demonstrably fails to bear this theory out. It must be seen that the roots of deficiency in this view extend far deeper than mere lack of access to ulterior realities. Instead, any observation of reality independent of mind succeeds in falsifying itself in principle before it can even be carried out. After all, where would the observations come from?

Still, a different objection could be raised by appeal to the multiverse hypotheses that are currently entertained by a number of prominent theoretical physicists. But to postulate something as a hypothesis to "save the paradigm" is a far cry from establishing it through observation and on the basis of evidence. Models are, in some instances, interchangeable with theories or paradigms but they are never interchangeable with evidence. Hence, to the one who is inclined to dismiss the immanence theory of mind in the world as superstition, it must be objected that the boot is on the other leg: ours is the only universe we know of, and consciousness is always already present in all of our knowledge of it. But what about the universes we don't know of? By now, the objection should be moot and perhaps even tiresome, for on what basis do we suspect the existence of these alternatives? If it is on the basis of evidence, we have seen that consciousness is already inherent in that evidence and hence, the existence of that evidence as such refutes what it is being marshaled in attempts to prove. If it is on the basis of no evidence, then whence does the objection arise in the first place? Because this is a book about Barfield's thought, we will leave for another occasion speculation over what motives ulterior to evidence may lead a person unflaggingly to maintain such a view in spite of the lack of evidence to substantiate it. Instead, we hope that the possibility of consciousness's status as a fundamental element of the universe has been set forth convincingly enough that readers who nevertheless harbor objections will not summarily dismiss arguments of Barfield that are established on this premise.

5

Final Participation

AT THE END OF the last chapter, we argued that consciousness belongs together with reality and further that reality cannot be understood so long as consciousness is regarded as an afterthought, or something accidental, like an epiphenomenon of material processes. Any account of the world remains incomplete so long as it fails to include the very thing that allows us to give an account of the world in the first place. We cannot conceptualize "the world" without implying our own conceptualization—both as substance and as act. Consciousness can be distinguished from the rest of reality but not divided from it, as Barfield was fond of pointing out. To attempt a division of consciousness and reality is akin to extracting a cube from a grain of salt. Naturally, it is possible to conceive of the cuboid shape of the salt crystal as something distinct from the concrete entity that embodies it. Myriad other abstractions are likewise possible, including "saltiness," "whiteness," "smallness," and so on. But the fact that the salt crystallizes into a cube must not be treated as something ulterior to the salt itself, as though the cuboid form were a sort of "epiphenomenon" of the real salt. Barfield's argument is very similar in respect to consciousness: we can contemplate consciousness in itself as an abstraction on one hand, and the world in itself as an abstraction, on the other. Nevertheless, any concrete perception of either of these elements already implies the existence of the other, and to treat the product of cognitive abstraction as an independent entity falls into the fundamental error that Whitehead memorably decried as "the fallacy of misplaced concreteness."[1] "Idolatry," in the sense that Barfield stipulates, can be usefully understood as the unconscious, collective habit of misplacing concreteness.[2] Therefore, despite that people often regard the objective world as something entirely independent of our thinking, a critical examination of the evidence at hand calls for a revolution in our conventional views of this subject. The latter are advanced under the banner of scientific objectivity but the standard is misleading, as we shall shortly see. After all, what evidence could ever be gathered to support the notion that the really real world is ulterior to our experience of it and is to be sought, rather, amidst speculative hypotheses and mathematical abstractions? Any evidence in favor of such a theory entail its already having entered our experience and having refuted the very theory it was intended to corroborate.

At this juncture, the constant temptation presents itself to enter into a dispute over the so-called "hard problem of consciousness."[3] But this would be, once again, to settle back into a more or less familiar circuit of dialectics that transpires entirely in the flatland of Onlooker Consciousness. Just as no summation of vectors in a plane will ever result in a vector leading outside of it, so no concatenation of arguments in a given mode of consciousness will result in a transformation into another. Beta thinking is like a door which, so long as it is not passed through in fact, functions in a manner indistinguishable from any other wall. But if argumentation and dialectics are regarded not for the conclusions they may eventually produce but rather in the energetic function that is their engine—as pure activity of thought—then our moment will be cast in an entirely different light. It is here that we will gesture towards the fruition of Barfield's thought, which is, at the same time, an invitation beyond it. A fruit also bears the seed for the next generation. Indeed, it is precisely this quality of evolutionary vision that lends Barfield's thought its characteristically refreshing and even restless signature even within the matrix of his sober and conscientious argumentation. Those familiar with Barfield's *corpus* will have surmised that the theme of this chapter is none other than the conscious collaboration with Christ in the economy of creation, which is to say, "Final Participation."

To make sense of the evolutionary potential latent in the present condition of consciousness, it may be useful to recall, in the first instance, that "creation" does not refer to the picture of the universe provided by contemporary physics. Indeed, the latter is perhaps best conceived as a constellation

---

1. Whitehead, *Science and the Modern World*, 52.

2. The subtitle of *Saving the Appearances* is none other than *A Study in Idolatry*.

3. Cf. David Chalmers, "Facing Up to the Problem of Consciousness" and Treinen, *Redemption of Thinking*, 10–45.

of "idols in Einsteinian spacetime," to paraphrase Barfield's turn of phrase from *Saving the Appearances*. The reasons for this were outlined at the end of the preceding chapter and alluded to at the outset of the present one. In brief, "creation" cannot refer to an idol; reality cannot be grasped through abstraction or juxtaposed against something more real. On the contrary, an adequate perception of the world is something that we attain by entering *more* comprehensively and energetically into our conscious experience and not by attempting to circumvent it. As tempting as it may be to substitute models for experience and abstractions for true encounters, the result is never what it promises. Consciousness is never truly left behind; the "view-from-nowhere" framework that is the ideal of modern scientific "objectivity" is a chimerical notion. It is impossible to refer to "the world" or to "reality" without simultaneously referring to the mind's own activity in conceiving and perceiving it as well as the phylogeny that they share together. In other words, it is superstitious to refer to an objective world outside of conscious-ness, for consciousness is not a container and hence nothing can be spatially "outside" of it. "External" is clearly a relational term whose only sense is in connection with its complement. What is the ostensibly "external world" external to? It might be proposed that the externality refers to the boundar-ies of one's corporal frame. But this is less feasible than it may superficially appear. If the meaning of such designations as "internal" and "external" were conceived in spatial terms, they would be rendered into purely relative desig-nations, since the inside of any given body is the outside of every other one. "A man may fish with the worm that hath eat of a king, and eat of the fish that hath fed of that worm."[4] "Whose objectivity?," we must ask in each case. That "internal" and "external" would be entirely reduced to relative spatial designations is of decisive significance because the reason to propose such a paradigm in the first place is the guarantee of overcoming the inherent relativism of subjectivity: bracketing away the subjective element promised to confer objectivity to phenomena. But as noted, the designations of "inter-nal" and "external" are not really objective at all, but relative. Hence, it makes no sense to posit an objective world made of matter while simultaneously conceding that this very designation implies the lack of objectivity. On top of this, "outside of my skin" is not at all what is meant by "the external world," since your own epidermis, not to mention your heart, brain, and liver, are as much a part of the physical world as the book you are reading or the chair on which you sit. A cursory thought experiment can confirm this fact with less mess and inconvenience than a surgical operation; it is therefore advisable, at least in this instance, to distinguish without dividing.

4. Shakespeare, *Hamlet*, IV.ii.

Evidently, the external world is not external to consciousness because it is in virtue of consciousness that we are able to posit an external world in the first place. If the external world were really external, how would we know about it? "Objectivity," no less than any other concept, presupposes the existence of a mind to conceive it. Lacking the power of conception, we are left with only what is immediately given to the physical senses, which in itself is nothing definite: "full of sound and fury/signifying nothing."[5] The question of objectivity, therefore, arises in the relation between consciousness and the world and not as a feature of the conjectural "world-in-itself." It is, of course, possible to write words like this in a grammatical sentence and relate that sentence logically to other such sentences, but that is hardly adequate evidence for the existence of such a world.

But that reality cannot be divided from consciousness does not entail any sort of solipsism because a distinction is not the same thing as a division. If consciousness could be divided from reality in a definitive sense, then whatever we were conscious of would not be real and whatever was real would remain unknown to us. But consciousness should not be understood as something outside of reality to begin with. In the last chapter, we attempted to illustrate their anterior unity and their coevolution from there. Reality divorced from consciousness is an abstract model of the world that is inconsistent with any concrete evidence that can be adduced from this one. When it is imagined that consciousness is left behind for the sake of apprehending objective reality in itself, in fact what has been achieved is that consciousness has been configured—and perhaps *disfigured*—in such a manner that all of our perceptions are unconsciously refracted through conceptual models that nominally deny the existence of the very thing on which they most essentially depend. The result of such attempts at circumventing perspective in the effort to grasp reality outside of experience is therefore never what it professes to be. Instead, such an approach merely ensures that our experience will no longer be direct but vicarious—*idolatrous,* even—and it becomes exceedingly difficult to extricate true perceptions from conjectures and extrapolations. Barfield invites us to take an approach that is the inverse of the abstract one. To wit, we must attempt to encounter reality directly through consciousness and not by attempting to evade it.

One may argue that Onlooker Consciousness was never bereft of this direct encounter between consciousness and reality to begin with, and hence wonder why any evolution past the former configuration would be necessary. But, again, a sustained reflection on this mode of thinking will reveal the reason for this exigency. Namely, the very structure of Onlooker

5. Shakespeare, *Macbeth*, V.v.

Consciousness ensures that every one of the mind's perceptions, including that of its own nature and essence, will be perennially undermined by doubt. The oscillation throughout the history of ideas between, on one hand, rationalism and idealism (which tend to reject the substantiality of the material world) and, on the other, empiricism and scientism (which tend to bracket or ignore the mind entirely) is a picture of Onlooker Consciousness's perpetual bad faith. In the first instance, the abstraction of consciousness is given primacy while in the second, this position is awarded to the abstraction of a material world outside of consciousness. But it is no more possible to arrive at concrete reality from a departure point in abstraction than it is for a river to flow upwards or to make wheat from bread. Far from guaranteeing scientific objectivity, therefore, Onlooker Consciousness tends everywhere towards a fugue of polarization into the extremes of detached solipsism or crude materialism. If mind is conceived as something entirely heterogeneous from the perceptible world and, at the same time, no attempt is made to overcome this dichotomy, then intimations of pervasive alterity will everywhere undermine the very foundations of the objective facts that one, to begin with, had intended to establish through having bracketed away all subjectivity from the scientific endeavor. These intimations will inevitably condense into agnostic doctrines that poison the well of scientific confidence. Indeed, when the connection between Onlooker Consciousness and the fundamental cognitive posture that it embodies is grasped, it will no longer appear as an accident but as a historical necessity that philosophical movements like medieval Nominalism, Cartesian skepticism, Humean empiricism, and Kantian idealism should have arrived exactly as they did in the course of history. As fallen leaves may be carried on the current of a brook, so the history of ideas is borne along by the evolution of consciousness.

But, as noted, Barfield laid out a possibility latent in this evolutionary current, which remains to be actualized through individual initiative. With modernity, the perceived heterogeneity of mind and reality has reached such a pitch that it is possible for thinking to be perceived as such. This is to say that thinking has become so abstract from concrete reality that it is now possible for thought to become an object of its own activity. Ordinarily, thinking is employed as a means to perceive other things but thinking itself proceeds unnoticed. However, direct reflection on thinking *per se* presents a new potentiality in the evolution of consciousness that was not yet present so long as vestiges of Original Participation were still retained. In the latter condition, thoughts were inseparable from things and phenomena; hence it was impossible to grasp thinking itself any more than light and color can be separated from visible surfaces. Indeed, it is precisely the abstract, subjective, and enervated nature of contemporary thought that bears this evolutionary potential in a seminal form. To the same degree that concrete beings are conceived as idols, thinking itself is also liberated from its original participation in them. This is why, at the end of *Saving the Appearances,* Barfield exclaims "*O felix eidolon!*" The reader will recall that "alpha thinking" refers to the activity of mind turned towards objects outside of itself. Conversely, the initial act of turning the mind upon itself, Barfield designated with the term "beta thinking." Indeed, while the ordinary habits of mind orient it to reflect on the objects of its perception, the mind may also reflect on objects of its own creation and finally, attempt to grasp its own free creativity in the very act. Thus, in contrast to alpha thinking, beta thinking indicates a configuration of the mind in which it takes its own thought as its object. In this way, alpha thinking and beta thinking at first can be said to refer to identical functions that are, to begin with, distinguished only in their objects. But the moment that beta thinking is performed, it reveals itself to be distinct from alpha thinking not only in content but also in form and in essence. The observation of one's own thinking is reflexive by nature. Alpha thinking, therefore, lacks an element that is present in its counterpart. In beta thinking, thought is turned upon itself and hence, it is self-aware. Ordinarily, thinking is directed toward objects ulterior to it but remains unaware of itself. In beta thinking, this posture is reordered such that the erstwhile unobserved element in experience enters into consciousness. And because this element is consubstantial with the thinking which grasps it, the first steps are taken towards overcoming the subject-object chasm that characterizes the state of Onlooker Consciousness. In this way, sustained engagement in beta thinking heralds a transfiguration of ordinary experience.

In the mode of alpha thinking, a person would be inclined to pose a question like "how does consciousness emerge from nonconscious matter?" If the question is pictured as a ball, alpha thinking can be likened to a dog that will give chase, ultimately to retrieve the ball and initiate the process all over again. But whereas alpha thinking is a dog, which will be inclined to chase what is thrown, beta thinking is a lion, which will not. Indeed, the very fact of having posed such a question demonstrates the possibility to turn about, as it were, and to apprehend one's own noetic activity, of which the question above was the final issue. The moment that the product of such an activity is indexed to its hidden source and origin, a revolution in consciousness is at hand. To retrace this current of cognition is to enter into a living experience of thinking; to go from grasping objects through thought to grasping thinking *eo ipso* as a self-evident and self-sustaining spiritual activity. As Rudolf Steiner wrote in regard to the reflexive observation of thinking:

> This then is indisputable, that in thinking we have got hold of
> one corner of the whole world process which requires our pres-
> ence if anything is to happen. And this is just the point upon
> which everything turns. The very reason why things confront
> me in such a puzzling way is just that I play no part in their
> production. They are simply given to me, whereas in the case of
> thinking I know how it is done. Hence for the study of all that
> happens in the world there can be no more fundamental start-
> ing point than thinking itself.[6]

In other words, beta thinking is a foothold that our minds can gain on their
journey to transcend the boundaries of Onlooker Consciousness.

We will presently attempt to unfold this insight further. To begin with,
it bears repeating that beta thinking is both the same and different from
alpha thinking. In a certain manner, beta thinking is identical to alpha
thinking in that both of them are accomplished by the same mental function. Thus alpha thinking and beta thinking are distinguished only in their
objects. At the same time, however, beta thinking is categorically distinct
from alpha thinking because only one of them is reflexive: only beta thinking has begun to lift into consciousness its own pathways and operations.
Because the object of beta thinking is its own products, it serves as a sort of
touchstone of certainty amidst the innumerable sources of error inherent in
alpha thinking. To wit, a person may doubt that his thinking is correctly applied to objects ulterior to it, but no one who is willing to attend to his own
mind may doubt the existence of his thinking itself. The facts of thinking
are susceptible to doubt but the fact of thinking is not. Indeed, to doubt the
fact of thinking could only be carried out through further thinking, which
one had ostensibly decided not to trust. The doubt itself could not be trusted
and hence one would arrive right back at the starting point of observation in
which thinking is self-evident. Precisely because of this reflexivity inherent
in beta thinking—in which the object of consciousness approaches identity
with its subject, in which facts are known through *creation* and not through
inference—it may also function as a bridge to establish a continuity between
ordinary consciousness and a different state of consciousness altogether.
The latter is precisely the state of consciousness that Barfield meant to indicate by the term "Final Participation."

We described Final Participation above as conscious collaboration with
Christ in the economy of creation. We also observed in the last chapter in our

6. Steiner, *Philosophy of Freedom,* chapter 3.

characterization of alpha thinking that its knowledge claims are systematically undermined by the Onlooker Consciousness of which it is a function. Because thinking in the mode of Onlooker Consciousness takes no account of its own role in its figurations, perception and conception are believed to bear no relation. Products of figuration confront Onlooker Consciousness as brute material objects that are wholly other in essence from the mind that perceives them. Hence, knowledge of these phenomena can only come about through inference. Let us explore this point. If we observe snow falling from the bough of a tree, we can infer the laws and circumstances that led to and defined this occurrence. But, of course, these are always subject to change, whether by (a) new observations or (b) new concepts.

As an example of the former (a), one may imagine that, upon further observation, a bird was noticed to have disturbed the snow that, after the initial observation, was presumed to have fallen spontaneously. Or perhaps one feels a breeze and postulates it as the cause. Or perhaps there were not one, but two birds. Or maybe it was a squirrel, or a yeti, and so on. There are virtually no limits to the quantity of possible causes that could be adduced to explain the falling snow provided that they all conform to the basic parameters of the scenario as grasped in our conception of it. But note that it is only in virtue of our higher-order concept of *causality*, which can be seen as a variation on the Principle of Sufficient Reason,[7] that we seek an explanation to begin with, just as it is only in virtue of our ordinary concepts that we are able to recognize pertinent instances of them in our general observations which are capable of meeting our expectation that the falling snow should have a cause. If we did not expect that events should have causes, we would not seek for them. Likewise, if we did not possess ordinary concepts, we wouldn't find such causes even if we did. Of course, any viable explanation must consist in the disclosure of an intelligible relationship between the phenomenon in question and other phenomena or ideas that are theoretically capable of explaining it or else we would not call it an explanation. It would not be adequate, for instance, to propose Kepler's Laws of Planetary Motion[8] as an explanation to the event above because we can't imagine how

7. Cf. Leibniz: "Our reasonings are grounded upon two great principles, that of contradiction, in virtue of which we judge false that which involves a contradiction, and true that which is opposed or contradictory to the false; And that of sufficient reason, in virtue of which we hold that there can be no fact real or existing, no statement true, unless there be a sufficient reason, why it should be so and not otherwise, although these reasons usually cannot be known by us." *Monadology*, paras. 31 and 32.

8. First Law: Planetary orbits are elliptical with the sun at a focus. Second Law: The radius vector from the sun to a planet sweeps equal areas in equal times. Third Law: The ratio of the square of the period of revolution and the cube of the ellipse semi-major axis is the same for all planets.

purely kinematic relationships could exert any material influence on any particular snow-laden branch.[9] We haven't specified what "breathes fire into the equations," so to speak.[10]

The above discussion may assist us in arriving at an understanding of the effect that new concepts (b) will have on our inferences about the cause of the falling snow. Indeed, our conception of the scenario is constituted by a comprehensive latticework of harmonious and interconnected concepts and it is only upon the hint of incongruity that we feel impelled to seek an explanation for anything to begin with. This was indicated above in reference to the concept of "causality" and the Principle of Sufficient Reason. As agitations in a spider's web alert the creature of a captive insect, so our familiar concepts extend through the phenomenal world like interwoven filaments suspended in a state of heightened sensitivity to the slightest disturbance in our expectation. By "snow," we understand a heap of inert substance. When, therefore, it appears to move of itself, the chords of our understanding are struck in an aspect of dissonance that at once impels our minds to wakeful activity as they seek to reconcile the apparent discord. If the snow were a dryad, no explanation would be necessary because dryads possess animate souls and are hence capable of endogenous locomotion. But because the snow remains itself and dryads do not seem to exist, the snow's sudden movement demands an explanation.

In essence, we recognize a satisfactory explanation by its ability to accommodate an observation without forfeiting conceptual coherence. It is crucial to grasp that it is only in virtue of our concept of "gravity" that we are able to understand how the agitation of a branch could function as a cause

9. It is interesting to note that Newton is often credited with completing the project that Kepler inaugurated by supplementing the latter's equations with an explanation of the dynamic counterparts. And yet, this is not entirely faithful to the historical facts of the matter. Newton, after all, when pressed as to the cause of the gravitational attraction that his Laws of Motion described, countered with the famous "hypothesis non fingo!" That is, "I don't hypothesize!" Thus, a dynamic explanation of celestial motion would have to wait until Einstein's Theory of General Relativity. It is worth wondering, however, whether the latter really explains anything at all. After all, it merely posits a relationship between mass and the curvature of spacetime. In other words, the mass of bodies is explained by curvature in the geodesic of spacetime and the curvature of the geodesic of spacetime is explained by the presence of massive bodies. If the example above was framed in a similar logical structure, it is unlikely that anyone would be satisfied: "the snow falls because of its heaviness and the snow is heavy because it falls."

10. Hawking, *Brief History of Time* (174): "Even if there is only one possible unified theory, it is just a set of rules and equations. What is it that breathes fire into the equations and makes a universe for them to describe? The usual approach of science of constructing a mathematical model cannot answer the questions of why there should be a universe for the model to describe. Why does the universe go to all the bother of existing?"

of snow falling from it. After all, without gravity, the snow, if loosed, would not fall. Moreover, it is illuminating to reflect on the manner by which revolutions in the scientific concept of "gravity" itself subtend one's conception of the entire gestalt in question. Prior to the late seventeenth or early eighteenth century, had anyone perceived the scenario described above and found himself posed with the question as to the cause of the snow's falling, he may have included *gravitas* in his explanation. But by this term, he would have been referring to a phenomenologically self-evident quality of the snow itself: namely, its weight or its heaviness. Thus, "the snow fell because of *gravitas*" would have been tantamount to saying that "the snow fell because it was heavy," as well as "the snow is heavy because it falls." This is not circular reasoning but rather an expression of the fact that heaviness was not thought of as something independent from an entity's inclination to fall. It is well known that Newton's universal theory of gravitation represented a revolution in the scientific conception of *gravitas*. "Heaviness" was no longer pictured as a quality inherent to a massive body but as a general force acting indiscriminately on all bodies throughout the universe. In Newton's conception, "every particle attracts every other particle in the universe with a force that is directly proportional to the product of their masses and inversely proportional to the square of the distance between their centers."[11] It can at once be observed that the Newtonian theory of universal gravitation implies an entirely different conception of what it means to say "the snow fell because it was heavy." Heaviness must be conceived not as a property that is immanent to the snow but one that arises as a force relationship between the "particles" in the snow and those of the planet, and by extension, all bodies in the universe.

By the same token, to integrate Einstein's General Relativity theory into one's picture of the innocent falling snow once again demands a reconception of our entire imaginary of what is at stake in the hypothetical scenario. Whatever the efficient cause of the snow's falling at the precise moment that it did, the reason that it should fall at all is no longer to be conceived as belonging to the snow itself. Nor, however, should it be imagined as a positive force exerting its influence upon the particles of snow that make up the heap in question. Instead, the apparent attraction that the earth brings to bear upon the snow when it is loosed from its bough is to be seen as a phenomenon that emerges from the local curvature in the geodesic of spacetime that the planet, and to a lesser extent, all massive bodies in the universe, produce in their vicinity. Hence, gravity is not really understood to be the cause of anything at all. Instead, the snow merely falls along the curvature of

11. Newton, *Principia,* Proposition 75, Theorem 35.

space through time in the same way that a nickel will follow the contours of one's pocket to arrive ultimately at the bottom. Everything simply falls along a straight path through curved spacetime. Newton had imagined a universal force propagating itself through uniform space. Einstein, by contrast, offers the view of relativistic spacetime, which is not absolute but which rather emerges as a function of relationships between massive bodies in a manner analogous to that by which a melodic interval between two tones generates musical "space" in their interval, which was not there before the melody carved it out. In other words, space does not preexist the phenomena that it surrounds—it is no longer conceptualized as a *container* but as a *topology*. The latter term, drawn from cartography and mathematics, also serves, in a sort of felicitous recursivity, to cast new light on our so-called "latticework" or "spider's web" of concepts. Through analogical vision, it can be seen that, just as massive bodies are understood to subsist amidst a topology of relativistic spacetime, so too are all of the concepts embedded in a comprehensive topology of intelligibility and meaning. "Space" alone cannot be reconceived without necessitating a reconception of "gravity," of "time," and virtually the entire paradigm of physics to boot through which we are picturing the innocuous scenario of snow falling from a branch.

We hope that the discussion above has served at once to disclose the cognitive activity that is inextricable from even the most rudimentary of observations as well as to demonstrate the contingency of the knowledge claims wrought by conventional processes of alpha thinking. After all, without thinking we would never know what we were observing and hence would not actually be observing at all. And if classical physics was reimagined by Einstein, there is no reason to expect that General Relativity will not one day give way to some new paradigm. Moreover, any conclusion arrived at through empirical observation is subject to falsification by further empirical observation.

But the first point above actually serves to deliver us from the problems that the second one brings to light. It is also to be hoped, therefore, that the above discussion will have successfully gestured towards a possibility to escape the *cul-de-sac* of alpha thinking and Onlooker Consciousness. If—through a foreground-background shift in our perception—we regard the entire above discussion not in regard to what it was attempting to demonstrate in respect to something other than itself, but rather in respect to the very internal dynamism of the thinking activity *per se,* which left the thoughts outlined above in its wake, we will find ourselves confronted with an entirely different phenomenon. Specifically, we will have "taken hold of one corner of the whole world process."[12] We will find ourselves in a situation in which our knowledge is begotten not through conjecture but through being—anyone who successfully navigated the arguments above has *performed* something in a very concrete, though not necessarily material, sense. Importantly, there is no need to infer the fact of this performance since the thinking movements were carried out by each person himself and thus, are known through a direct intuition that can be compared to kinaesthetic or proprioceptive knowledge. One may lift one's hand and look at it, or imagine how it would look to someone else. But one can also lift one's hand in the dark and experience the movement inwardly—not in space, but in time. It is the latter approach that provides the best analogy to what we may strive for in respect to thinking. Regarding the falling snow: we were forced to attempt to arrive at the causes of the event through inference from its effects. But in respect to the kinaesthetic activity of our own thinking, we encounter an objective occurrence of which we experience its cause and principle in unmediated intuition. Indeed, we recognize our own "I" to be the agent cause of the thinking activity. From here, we may grasp the coherence of the latter with its further effects in our familiar thoughts and perceptions. We know intuitively that the thinking activity is our own deed and hence, so too do we recognize our own responsibility for the thoughts that this immediate activity of thinking produces. Final Participation is to trace these thoughts back to the spiritual activity which sent them forth and thence to experience directly our own living participation in the chorus of creation; it is to grasp the manner in which our conscious thoughts are the issue of our thinking which, in turn, issues forth from our "I" as its deed. Hence, Final Participation is also self-knowledge in the truest sense.

In this manner, it can be seen that what Christ the Logos is to creation, so is the "I" in respect to its own thinking: "Have I not said Ye are gods? If he called them gods, unto whom the *logos* of God came, and the scripture cannot be broken."[13] Thus, Final Participation can be seen as a progressive realization of the *imago Dei*[14] in Man. Indeed, Saint Jerome, credited with the Latin Vulgate translation of the Old Testament, elected to render the original Hebrew text, familiar in English translations as "in our image," not as *in imagine nostra,* but as *ad imaginem nostrum,* which is to say, "*towards*" and not "*in* our image." In other words, to bear the image of God is something to be achieved through an evolutionary process. Barfield's

12. Steiner, *Philosophy of Freedom,* ch. 3.

13. John 10:34–35.

14. Genesis 1:26–27.

assertion that "Christ is the cosmic wisdom on its way from Original to Final Participation"[15] can spring to life in light of this connection. Indeed, Final Participation is the experience of knowledge through spiritual creation and creation through direct and intuitive knowledge.[16]

For another perspective on Final Participation, let us consider how instincts work in us and compare what we discover to similar observations we can make in respect to abstract reasoning. In the first instance, we may observe that the contents are, in a certain respect, our own doing. At the same time, however, the agency behind them is unconscious. As a result, these contents are ultimately known *a posteriori* in the same manner as any other natural phenomenon, like the hypothetical falling snow, for instance, as described above. In other words, in both the function of our instincts and the falling snow, the object or event in question *precedes* our consciousness of it. If a gun is fired, first I blink and then I know that I have blinked. Because of this, we find ourselves at the epistemological disadvantage of having to infer from perceived effects to causes that we do not know and can only conjecture. After all, the blink may have only happened to follow the sound in time but in fact have sprung from entirely different causes. Still, I know that it was I who blinked despite that I cannot be certain why.

If we next consider abstract reasoning, we may observe a fruitful contrast with the instinctive functions. As noted earlier in this discussion, however, we will also encounter the familiar problem of knowledge that is endemic to Onlooker Consciousness. An example of this approach was offered above in our attempts to grasp the cause of the falling snow. Recall that in the case of instinctive functions, the deed was ours but it was performed outside of consciousness. In the case of abstract reasoning, by contrast, despite that its results are conscious to us, there is no perceptible *deed* on our behalf other than the cognitive one, which we infer, of establishing a logical relationship between two natural occurrences but which, as indicated, ordinarily escapes our notice because it is overshadowed

15. Barfield, *Saving Appearances*, 185.

16. Cf. St. Maximos the Confessor: "If God made all things by His will (cf. Rev 4:11), and it is always pious and right to say that God knows His own will, and that He made each creature by an act of will, then God knows existing things as He knows the products of His own will, since He also made existing things by an act of will. Furthermore, I think that these assertions are in accord with what is said in the Scripture to Moses: 'I know you above all' (Ex. 18:11). And about some it was said: 'The Lord knows those who are His' (II Tim. 2:19). And to others He said: 'I do not know you' (Mt. 7:23; 15:12). Voluntary movement, either in accord with the will and word of God or against the will and word of God, prepared each person to hear the divine voice." *On the Cosmic Mystery of Jesus Christ.*

by its results. Thus, we find ourselves in the characteristic posture of the Onlooker Consciousness engaged in alpha thinking about figurations and ideas in whose coming to be it pretends to have played no part. While the instinctive functions proceed outside of our self-conscious awareness, the logical relationships that we elaborate through alpha thinking are clear and manifest to consciousness. Moreover, we are aware that those relationships cannot manifest themselves without our having thought them. Hence, through alpha thinking, we are also moved toward self-consciousness. In the first instance, it can therefore be said, *participation* is present without *self-consciousness* while in the second instance *self-consciousness* is present without *participation*. In the first case, the action is our own but the reason was not while in the second, the reason is ours but the object was something unrelated to us. These moments represent, in a sort of hologram, the phylogenetic states of Original Participation and Onlooker Consciousness, respectively.

Suppose, however, a third scenario for which our own thinking serves as the paradigmatic case. In respect to an observation of our own thinking, the phenomenon in question is nothing outside of itself. We can consider, for instance, the very noetic activity that we leveraged in order to elaborate the arguments above *irrespective* of whether the conclusions that this activity produced be correct relative to other phenomena or not. The point is not to arrive at erroneous judgments but rather to concentrate our noetic activity to a pitch. This is accomplished by taking up the act of thinking while bracketing away, to begin with, all sources of its dissipation, including doubts as to its conformity to an ulterior standard of correctness. Insofar as we are measuring the conclusions of our thinking activity against something other than itself, our attention has been distracted from the point at issue, which is precisely the concentration of thinking activity upon its own energy. In this concentration, we have changed the subject to the first point at which we can find a true and indisputable epistemic foothold. Initially, our awareness does not encompass the activity of thinking because the former was magnetized by the perceptions, conclusions, thoughts, doubts, and judgments that are the products of this activity. But we can infer the presence of this activity because otherwise none of these products would appear for us and we would be left dumb and insensate. At any moment, therefore, it is possible to effect the foreground-background shift alluded to above and awaken to thinking *in actu*. In this way, self-consciousness is kindled within participation and participation irradiated with self-consciousness. The contrast between the Onlooker state and the higher consciousness can be symbolized in Christ's ability to walk on water. Peter[17] and the other disciples, by contrast, symbolize the typical state of Onlooker Consciousness and alpha thinking, which must cling to their Petrine concepts and representations without any awareness of the living waters from which those representations went forth. Hence, the disciples could only set foot on dry land; while at sea, they required an extraneous vessel lest they be submerged in the chaotic and metamorphosing waters. In the same way, alpha thinking operates within the vessel of Onlooker Consciousness, which serves to keep this thinking afloat but which also isolates it from any direct contact with reality. To symbolize Original Participation in this analogy, we would perhaps have to look to the fishes. But one thing is clear: that in Final Participation, we close the circuit, as it were, between the alternating polarities of *participation* and *consciousness*. Put another way, Final Participation is a sort of *coniunctio oppositorum*—a sacred marriage between these erstwhile sundered poles.

Because consciousness no longer stands in opposition to participation, the primary activity of consciousness in Final Participation is no longer ordinary thinking, whose function was, by definition, to reconcile, through cognition, the subject-object dichotomy that characterized the Onlooker state. Just as figuration is something other—and arguably more "poetic" in the original meaning of that term—than ordinary thinking, so too is the new thinking, which is irradiated by the light of consciousness and performed by the agency of the "I," something more than what we have conventionally understood by the term. All of the phenomena whose exteriors were familiar to us through Onlooker Consciousness can be rediscovered from the side of their creativity and life: like is known by like,[18] and thinking, participated finally, is a free and creative act. We may have followed the letter of Barfield's scheme and gone on to designate the intensified thinking activity by the proximate character in the Greek alphabet. But in the spirit of Barfield's vision, we will instead invoke a more iconic nomenclature. The phenomenon we have known as mere "thinking," when

17. I.e., "The Rock," since the given name "Peter" is from the Greek Πέτρος, *Petros.*

18. Cf. Aristotle's *De Anima* 404b, where he ascribes the view to Empedocles and Plato ("γινώσκεσθαι γὰρ τῷ ὁμοίῳ τὸ ὅμοιον"). Presumably, the *loci classici* are Empedocles's Fragment 106:
For it is by Earth that Earth we see; by Water, Water,
By Ether, Ether divine; by Fire, destructive Fire;
By Love Love, and Hate by cruel Hate.
And Plato's *Timaeus* 45a: "So whenever the stream of vision is surrounded by midday light, it flows out like unto like, and coalescing therewith it forms one kindred substance along the path of the eyes' vision, wheresoever the fire which streams from within collides with an obstructing object without."

participated finally, reveals itself to have been, already from the very begin-ning—from the first stirrings of self-conscious thought—a participation in the incarnation of Christ. Christ says, "I am . . . the end and the beginning, the first and the last."[19] Let the final participation of thinking be known, then, as "omega thinking."

19. Cf. Revelation 22:13: "I am Alpha and Omega, the beginning and the end, the first and the last."

6

Science, Technology, and the Crisis of Meaning

IN THIS FINAL CHAPTER, we will briefly explore one of the many ways in which Barfield's insights into human language and the evolution of consciousness can be "put to work." Regrettably, though in a manner entirely consistent with Barfield's theories, philosophy, as the discipline is commonly understood today, has been stripped of its substance and scope over the centuries since its inception in ancient Athens. The "ivory tower" academic who teaches metaphysics as a day job and then does not give the subject a second thought after he leaves the office is very far from the powerful ideal that the title of "philosopher" once evoked. Plato affirmed that keeping the company of wisdom should lend wings to the mind of the philosopher,[1] and Thoreau, protesting the professionalization of philosophy, aimed to recover its older sense: "To be a philosopher," he wrote, "is not merely to have subtle thoughts, nor even to found a school, but so to love wisdom as to live according to its dictates, a life of simplicity, independence, magnanimity and trust."[2] Similarly, in *Surprised by Joy*, C. S. Lewis recalled a time when he was lunching with Barfield and a mutual friend, Griffiths: "I happened to refer to philosophy as 'a subject.' 'It wasn't a subject to Plato,' said Barfield,

---

1. Plato, *Phaedrus*, 246.
2. Thoreau, *Walden*, 14.

'it was a way.'"[3] Barfield, it seems, never lost touch with the ancient ideal of philosophy, which Plato so eloquently portrays in the *Republic*:

> just as the eye was unable to turn from darkness to light without the whole body, so too the instrument of knowledge can only by the movement of the whole soul be turned from the world of becoming into that of being, and learn by degrees to endure the sight of being, and of the brightest and best of being, or in other words, of the good.[4]

We hope, in doing so, to provide at least a hint at its immense explanatory power. The subject at hand is the historical phenomenon that has lately been dubbed "the modern crisis of meaning." Needless to say, "the meaning crisis," despite not yet having received that title in Barfield's day, is a theme that was of immense personal and intellectual importance to him. Barfield expressed his concern for this crisis in the following words:

> Amid all the signs that surround us in the middle of the twentieth century, perhaps the one which fills thoughtful people with the greatest foreboding is the growing general sense of meaninglessness. It is this that underlies most other threats. How is it that the more able man becomes to manipulate the world to his advantage, the less he can perceive any meaning in it?[5]

Thus, Barfield's understanding of the matter can be usefully encapsulated in two propositions: first, that there has been and continues to be a growing sense of meaninglessness, at least in the West, and second, that there is a strong connection between the crisis of meaning and Western society's ever-increasing ability to manipulate the natural world to serve human ends.

Writers who have commented on the "growing general sense of meaninglessness" that represents such a salient feature of the modern age are as many and varied as are the exegeses they offer as to the causes and consequences thereof. It is true that some have opined that a sense of meaninglessness is perennial and can only be said to manifest itself differently in each new era than it had in those prior. In other words, meaninglessness is a perennial hallmark of human existence that endures in essence in spite of continual adventitious inflections by historical circumstance. Such thinkers, in Barfield's words, attribute it to "a fundamental perversity, a sort of 'pure

---

3. Lewis continued: "The quiet but fervent agreement of Griffiths, and the quick glance of understanding between these two, revealed to me my own frivolity." Lewis, *Surprised by Joy*, 225.

4. Plato, *Republic*, 518c.

5. Barfield, "Rediscovery of Meaning," in *Rediscovery of Meaning and Other Essays*, 13.

cussedness,' in human nature."[6] Though these are few in number, fewer still are the thinkers who argue that modernity can be uniquely characterized by the spontaneous perception of meaning inherent in the world. Most modern writers have recognized the present condition as the fallout of a historical process, at the outset of which, in C. S. Lewis's words, "the universe appears packed with will, intelligence, life and positive qualities; every tree is a nymph and every planet a god."[7] Over time, it is often asserted, "[t]he advance of knowledge gradually empties this rich and genial universe: first of its gods, then of its colours, smells, sounds and tastes, finally of solidity itself as solidity was once imagined."[8] All qualitative aspects of nature have, so it is alleged, been "debunked" and explained away by modern philosophy and science in terms of quantitative physical processes. Accordingly, the concept of "the world" today appears, to these observers, to encompass at once considerably less and more than pre-modern societies would have grasped with the term: the explosion in the universe's physical size has occurred in inverse proportion to an implosion in its significance. In the words of Peter Kreeft, there is a growing consensus among many that "[t]hought is only cerebral biochemistry, love is only lust, man is only a 'trousered ape,' religion is only myth, consciousness is only an epiphenomenon of matter, life is only the candle's brief and pointless sputter between two infinite expanses of darkness."[9] The world external to the individual modern human mind has, consequently, been emptied of all perceivable significance. Postmodernism, with its increasing emphasis on subjective experience as the sole ground of meaning, has largely been born out of this failure of modern thought and culture to say anything of true spiritual import. It is not obvious, however, that postmodernism has brought any significant improvement in this regard. Instead, it seems merely to have undermined our faith in the ability to participate in shared objective meanings and led to an increasing fragmentation of society into "watertight compartments." Needless to say, the process of fragmentation tends ineluctably towards a state of arbitrariness and solipsism as each compartment continues to divide into smaller and smaller units. But far from delivering us from a condition of meaninglessness, such a condition promises its fruition. After all, it is not clear that meaning, like language, must not necessarily transcend mere subjectivity to be at all. Indeed, it is hard to imagine how anything could be meaningful that did not, in some way, extend beyond itself. It is precisely the manner

6. Barfield, "Rediscovery of Meaning," in *Rediscovery of Meaning and Other Essays*, 13.

7. Lewis, "Empty Universe," in *Present Concerns*, 103.

8. Lewis, "Empty Universe," in *Present Concerns*, 103.

9. Kreeft, *C. S. Lewis and the Third Millennium*, 166.

by which it provides for an intersubjective participation in meaning that language is, well, *meaningful,* and it is doubtful that a language with a single speaker would be a language in anything but name only.[10] As Wittgenstein once quipped, "If a lion could speak, we could not understand him."[11]

As shown above, Barfield, Lewis, and others have noted that the ability to perceive meaning in the cosmos is often understood to be, historically speaking, directly proportional to the supposed ignorance of prior ages, and inversely proportional to the amount that is now known about the world through science. The story is most often told as follows: ancient humans lived in ignorance of the actual causes of natural phenomena and, being ruled by fear and superstition, projected the dynamics of their own psyches onto the outer world, anthropomorphizing all things and contriving to see will and agency behind everything that happened. Eons of superstitious animism elapsed before, almost of a sudden, people were delivered from their primitive beliefs by the advent of the scientific method. In Alexander Pope's famous epitaph for Isaac Newton's tombstone: "Nature and nature's laws lay hid in Night. / God said, 'Let Newton be!' and all was light." Following the Scientific Revolution, conventionally scientific explanations began to replace people's superstitious belief in "personified causes," to borrow a famous phrase from Edward Tylor.[12] Therefore, as science has expanded human knowledge about nature, human *perception* of nature has been supposedly freed from the conditioning influence of false beliefs, resulting in nature itself being revealed as nothing more than a spiritless collection of material objects moving in conformity to fixed causal laws. This narrative, or one much like it, has indelibly stamped itself on a number of crucial disciplines, including psychology and anthropology, and has found its way to a seemingly permanent place in the Western imaginary through the work of popularizers of science and history.

As we have indicated in prior chapters, Barfield found the assumptions behind this account largely unconvincing and questioned a number of its premises and evidential underpinnings. For example, he questioned the assumption that the historical progression from ancient to contemporary times can be understood in terms of simple, unidirectional progress from ignorance to knowledge. He pointed out, for instance, that the discernable

10. And the name would necessarily have to be understood more commonly, by the same token, to be a name and not just a noise.

11. Wittgenstein, *Philosophical Investigations,* 223.

12. The tendency to personify causes was Tylor's way of explaining the creation of mythology: "First and foremost among the causes which transfigure into myth the facts of daily experience, is the belief in the animation of all nature, rising at its highest pitch to personification." *Primitive Culture,* 258.

history of the human mind is best characterized in a manner that is exactly
the opposite of what the theory above would predict. Far from depicting
an expansion of consciousness, recorded history seems instead to portray a
narrowing of it. In other words Barfield resisted the popular characterization of history as "man getting to know more and more about more and
more," in favor of a more subtle account: that is, "man getting to know more
and more about less and less."[13] We noted above how our conception of
"philosophy," as such, has followed precisely this trajectory. Making the
same point with specific reference to the differences between modern and
pre-modern knowledge, Barfield wrote that "[t]he Aristotelean age that
preceded the scientific revolution was infantile compared to our own in the
accuracy of its knowledge. But it was adult compared to our own in the *scope*
of it."[14] As Barfield saw it, human knowledge has not necessarily grown except in one particular respect: what we usually call "scientific knowledge."[15]
But scientific knowledge is only one form of knowledge and, according to
Barfield, it has not been merely *added* to the sum total of human knowledge
but *purchased at the expense of other forms:* "Our sophistication, like Odin's,
has cost us an eye."[16] The growth in scientific knowledge has come with a
significant cost: a contraction of human consciousness.

Objections to the characterization above suggest a standpoint firmly
rooted in a scientific hegemony sometimes referred to as "scientism."
Broadly speaking, scientism can be characterized as the view that no proposition can be true unless it is, in principle at least, verifiable by scientific
inquiry. Or, in a more rigorous form, scientism is the view that the scope of
scientific inquiry is coextensive with reality as such. But Barfield saw clearly
what has since become more widely recognized: to wit, that scientism in
any of its forms is untenable for the simple reason that its own principle

---

13. Barfield, "Rediscovery of Meaning," in *Rediscovery of Meaning and Other Essays,*
22–23.

14. Barfield, *History, Guilt, and Habit,* 75. Our emphasis.

15. This designation generally encompasses the sort of knowledge that can be gained
from empirical observation and controlled experimentation, though circumscribing
the denotation of it is exceedingly problematic. After all, none of the discoveries in the
last century and a half of physics has been perceptible to the human senses. Instead,
every one of these discoveries represents an inference as to imperceptible causes of
perceptible phenomena. In other words, they represent "likely stories" enlisted for the
sake of, well, saving the appearances. The majority of scientific work today consists
in the elaboration of computer models to extrapolate from definite measurements to
larger trends. Of course, the situation presents the risk that models, which are theories
translated into functional algorithms, begin to be regarded as facts and hence employed
as substitutions for actual observation.

16. Barfield, *Poetic Diction,* 87.

contradicts its purport. The proposition that "All knowledge is, at least in principle, verifiable by scientific inquiry" cannot be so verified and so, *quod erat demonstrandum,* cannot be known. There are so many elements in common experience that remain entirely inexplicable in exclusively scientific terms that it is somewhat of a wonder that the scientistic axiom could ever catch on.[17] Moreover, as noted, no observation or controlled experiment could, even in principle, prove scientism is true because of the very internal contradiction that its formulation implies. In short, scientism is self-defeating because it fails to meet its own criterion of validity. For Barfield, therefore, scientism and similar views fall among the substantial number of contemporary philosophies that, for similar reasons, have little to recommend them.[18]

In the nineteenth century, a particularly stringent form of scientism known as "the positive philosophy" and later simply as "positivism" rose to prominence. Positivism, in its more zealous manifestation (most significantly represented by the logical positivism of the famous "Vienna circle"), asserts that propositions that cannot be verified empirically are not merely without truth-value, but *meaningless.* By the time Barfield began writing, the star of logical positivism had begun to wane. But many later critics of that philosophy had implicitly maintained one of its essential premises, leading to a version of epistemic, rather than ontological, scientism. In this view, the scope of scientific inquiry is coextensive, not necessarily with reality, but with *knowledge,* or, at least, "objective" knowledge. This view finds representative expression in the words of Bertrand Russell:

> While it is true that science cannot decide questions of value, that is because they cannot be intellectually decided at all, and lie outside the realm of truth and falsehood. Whatever knowledge

---

17. "Scientism" is a term that Barfield used almost interchangeably with terms such as "positivism" and "materialism," especially when their adoption was motivated by the desire to uphold a commitment to scientific inquiry as the sole method by which knowledge of the world can be attained. See, for example, his essay "Coming Trauma of Materialism," anthologized in *Rediscovery of Meaning and Other Essays.*

18. Barfield humorously disparaged such common failings of contemporary philosophies as follows: "It is a failing common of a good many metaphysical theories that they can be applied to all things except themselves but that, when so applied, they extinguish themselves, and experience has taught me that, when men are really attached to such a theory, most of them will, after it has been pointed out to them, continue nevertheless to apply it to all things (except itself)." *Poetic Diction,* 16. Such philosophies, he thought, are analogous to bayonets: What needs to be learned, he said, is "that you can do anything with bayonets except sit on them." *Poetic Diction,* 32.

is attainable, must be attained by scientific methods; and what
science cannot discover, mankind cannot know.[19]

The pervasiveness of this view has resulted in one of the most distinctive
features of postmodern culture: that is, the assumption that there are no
"facts" in the realm of value (morality, aesthetics, etc.). This split between
fact and value can usefully be understood as part of what Barfield called
"the residue of unresolved positivism," (or sometimes just R.U.P.) for it is
often tacitly affirmed even where positivism and related philosophies, like
scientism, have been explicitly denied.[20] Modern people are, thus, adrift in
an atmosphere of subconscious reductionism, even when such views are
consciously repudiated, for the reductionistic habit "lingers on in the [mod-
ern] imagination after it has been rejected by the intellect."[21] Thus, Barfield
observed, "even those who reject materialism as an ultimate philosophy
have been content to accept limitations which positivism seeks to impose
on the sphere of knowledge." The passage continues:

> True, they say, the spiritual values which constitute the true
> meaning of life can be dimly felt and are, in fact, what lies be-
> hind the symbols of religion and the mysterious phenomena of
> art. But we can never know anything about them. . . . There are
> . . . two kinds of truth: the scientific kind which can be dem-
> onstrated experimentally and which is limited to the physical
> world and, on the other side, the "truths" of mystical intuition
> and revelation, which can be felt or suggested but never known
> or scientifically stated.[22]

Unfortunately, those who have accepted this restriction in epistemology
have unwittingly admitted defeat in the realm of metaphysics, for science
will appear (if aforementioned assumptions are taken for granted) to reduce
the world on the other end of the distinctively modern Cartesian divide
between mind and matter to be a collection of inert objects, fully describ-
able in quantitative and mechanistic terms. Consistency demands that this
same method eventually be applied to the human mind, which must necessarily then be reduced to the physical brain and explained away as one more
object among objects, working blindly in accordance with the unchanging
laws of nature.

19. Russell, *Religion and Science*, 243.
20. Barfield, *History, Guilt, and Habit*, 67.
21. Barfield, *History, Guilt, and Habit*, 67.
22. Barfield, "Rediscovery of Meaning," in *Rediscovery of Meaning and Other Essays*,
15.

Thus, the denial of any "inside" to nature leads inexorably to the denial of an "inside" to human beings: "The meaning of a process is the inner being which the process expresses. The denial of any such being to the processes of nature leads inevitably to the denial of it to man himself."[23] And, as before, where a belief is preserved in something like a human mind or soul, the logic of scientism leads to the conclusion that nothing important about it can be known. In Barfield's words, "if physical objects and physical causes and effects are all that we can know, it follows that man himself can be known only to the extent that he is a physical object among physical objects."[24] Barfield concludes, therefore, that under the most distinctively modern assumptions, a person cannot "know anything about his specifically human self— his own inner being—any more than he can really know anything about the meaning of the world of nature by which he is surrounded."[25] Lewis made a similar observation about the trajectory of human self-understanding since the Scientific Revolution:

> The same method that has emptied the world [of meaning] now proceeds to empty ourselves. The masters of the method soon announce that we were just as mistaken (and mistaken in much the same way) when we attributed "souls," or selves or "minds" to human organisms, as when we attributed Dryads to the trees.[26]

They have concluded, he said, that "[w]e who have personified all things, turn out to be ourselves mere personifications."[27]

The specific sort of knowledge that has been gained since the Scientific Revolution is what Barfield called "dashboard knowledge," which is not knowledge of things *per se*, but of what "works." Naturally, "works" is defined as a function of the entire materialist paradigm in which the question is being posed. In other words, knowledge does not "work" in respect to refining the soul, as Plato may have defined it, or in terms of dying to the self to live

---

23. Barfield, "Rediscovery of Meaning," in *Rediscovery of Meaning and Other Essays*, 14.

24. Barfield, "Rediscovery of Meaning," in *Rediscovery of Meaning and Other Essays*, *14*.

25. Barfield, "Rediscovery of Meaning," in *Rediscovery of Meaning and Other Essays*, 14–15.

26. Lewis, "Empty Universe," in *Present Concerns,* 104.

27. Lewis, "Empty Universe," in *Present Concerns,* 104.

in Christ, to borrow the image from the Pauline epistles.[28] The measure of scientific knowledge is evidently not whether it brings the soul into closer communion with truth or with God. Instead, scientific knowledge is defined teleologically within a utilitarian matrix as anything that increases pleasure and material prosperity: "But the real and legitimate goal of the sciences is the endowment of human life with new inventions and riches," to quote the Lord Chancellor himself.[29] Barfield attempts to resensitize his readers to this definition of knowledge, which many have unconsciously inherited from the Baconian tradition, by characterizing it as "dashboard knowledge." The meaning of this term is best illustrated in a parable from *Saving the Appearances*. Barfield invites us to imagine a boy who has never seen a car and yet is placed inside of one. This boy sees all kinds of buttons, levers, pedals, and a steering wheel. Slowly, by experimenting, the boy figures out how to drive the car and uses it to get himself where he needs to go. He knows which buttons and pedals to press and release, and in what sequence, in order to procure his desired results. It will be obvious to the reader that the boy possesses an operational knowledge but not a comprehensive one. He understands nothing of fossil fuels, mechanics, Henry Ford, internal combustion, or the principles of physical engineering that make everything work as it does.[30] This boy's "dashboard knowledge" is practical and effective according to certain measures, just as modern knowledge of nature is practical and effective. At the same time, however, it is ultimately spurious. Indeed, the boy knows next to nothing of cars themselves, except how to make them do his bidding! If he assumes that, because his knowledge "works" according to the myopic conception of utility that he has chosen to entertain, his knowledge is complete, he will remain forever ignorant of everything else because, as Plato has reminded us in so many ways, the pretense of knowledge is the

---

28. "I am crucified with Christ: nevertheless I live; yet not I, but Christ liveth in me: and the life which I now live in the flesh I live by the faith of the Son of God, who loved me, and gave himself for me." Ephesians 2:20.

29. Cf. Bacon's full statement from the aphorisms of the *Novum Organum*, §LI: "There is another powerful and great cause of the little advancement of the sciences, which is this; it is impossible to advance properly in the course when the goal is not properly fixed. But the real and legitimate goal of the sciences is the endowment of human life with new inventions and riches." Bacon makes a similar statement shortly thereafter in §LXXI: "Nor must we omit the opinion, or rather prophecy, of an Egyptian priest with regard to the Greeks, that they would forever remain children, without any antiquity of knowledge or knowledge of antiquity; for they certainly have this in common with children, that they are prone to talking, and incapable of generation, their wisdom being loquacious and unproductive of effects. Hence the external signs derived from the origin and birthplace of our present philosophy are not favorable." *Novum Organum*, 348.

30. Barfield, *Saving the Appearances*, 55.

greatest barrier to wisdom. Barfield argued that, in general, ancient people and most living in the West up until the decline of the Middle Ages were primarily concerned with "engine knowledge," metaphorically speaking, and it has been only since the dawn of the modern era that people's concern has shifted to acquiring "dashboard knowledge."[31] In other words, up until the onset of modernity, people did not, as a rule, measure knowledge against utility but against truth.

The connection, then, between the advance of technology and the extenuation of perceived meaning is apparent from the fact that dashboard "knowledge" excludes meaning by the very way it defines the term. For this reason, it must be emphasized that modern reductionistic philosophies did not themselves induce the meaning crisis. Instead, such philosophies and the crisis of meaning have arisen from the same source and are, hence, expressions of the same underlying phenomenon. That phenomenon is the evolution of consciousness, which has configured the modern mind in such a way as to facilitate the advent of the more proximate cause of both the reductionistic philosophies and the meaning crisis: *viz.*, the collective mental habit of neglecting to attend to anything that is not empirical and reducible to physical processes and their effects—a habit that has been growing rapidly since the Scientific Revolution and has been spurred on by the almost unfathomable success of human technological advancement. The aforementioned philosophies took root in modern soil because the astonishing success of science and technology caused people to collapse the distinction between utility and truth.

As we have seen in earlier chapters, Barfield traced the history of human consciousness to an earlier time in which scientific knowledge was largely absent, but also in which another kind of knowledge characterized human thought and perception. This knowledge was born out of that vital connection between the human mind and the phenomena of nature (that is, "participation"). From this observation, Barfield developed an understanding of the ancient mind and the pre-modern perception of meaning in nature. What does it mean to say that ancient minds perceived nature as inherently meaningful? How is it that the inner life of nature was so naturally apparent when, for many moderns, it is only the "outside" of nature that is easily perceived?

Contrary to standard accounts of history accepted by many anthropologists, psychologists, and others, Barfield did not believe that meaning

31. Barfield, *Saving the Appearances*, 55.

was "projected" onto the world by ancient people, but that those communities saw *through* the outer appearances of the natural world into its soul; that the world outside of the human mind was, for them, not merely a collection of lifeless material objects and processes that had been falsely anthropomorphized, but a collection of living symbols in which a person's mind must understand through relationship. As participation has faded, then, the sense of meaninglessness has become more acute. Put another way, participation and meaninglessness form a polarity.

The idea of "seeing through" nature is worth elaborating because it further illuminates an interesting aspect of participatory consciousness. Barfield makes several different attempts at this elaboration in his writing. What does it mean to say that the outer forms of nature, which appear now to be inert and meaningless, were once "seen through," or perceived as outer expressions of inner significance? First, Barfield appealed to the places in which the inner significance of natural appearances is still easily perceived. For example, the human body, and particularly the human face, are still easily seen as outer expressions of inner meaning. All that is perceived with the senses when one encounters another person is material, "[b]ut in this case I know very well that the particular matter I am perceiving (the particular phenomenon) . . . is the expression . . . of another individual being."[32] He goes on to say that "what is important is not the relation between two phenomena as such . . . but the relation between two individual spirits, of which those bodies are reciprocally the vehicle and expression."[33] Where this is true of the body in general, it is particularly true of the face—the part of the body that George MacDonald fittingly described as "that living eternally changeful symbol which God has hung in front of the unseen spirit."[34] A person's face is still immediately perceived (without need for inference) as an expression of something more than the material of which it is composed. It is not properly said that a person's teeth are *actually* calcium and phosphorus, etc. Instead, it should be said that calcium and phosphorus are *actually* teeth, in this case, though they may have *potentially* become other things. More generally, the mode of perception engaged when one person sees the face of another is the vestigial remains of a mode of perception that, in former times, pervaded all human perception.

Another example of participation can be culled from the life of the English poet William Blake. In an exchange of correspondence with one of

32. Barfield, "Matter, Imagination and Spirit," in *Rediscovery of Meaning and Other Essays*, 216.

33. Barfield, "Matter, Imagination and Spirit," in *Rediscovery of Meaning and Other Essays*, 216.

34. MacDonald, "Imagination."

his contemporaries, Blake, when asked whether, when the sun rose, he did not perceive "a round disc of fire, somewhat like a guinea" responded as follows: "Oh! No! No! I see an innumerable company of the heavenly host, crying, 'Holy, holy, holy, is the Lord God almighty!'"[35] Blake was not, of course, giving a materially literal description of what he saw, but he rejected the modern prejudice that statements can only be true insofar as they are *literally* true in this way: "I question not my Corporeal or Vegetative Eye, any more than I would Question a Window concerning a Sight I look thro it and not with it."[36] Nor was the sun, for Blake, merely a convenient metaphor for the glory of God; it was, rather, a real expression of such, just as an unconscious smile is not a mere simile but a real expression of human happiness.

In another attempt—one that will best serve to illustrate the connection between modern consciousness and the crisis of meaning—Barfield suggests that pre-modern people saw the world in a way analogous to a person reading text on a page. "Now there is usually little connection between the physical causes of a thing and its meaning. An important physical cause of what I am just now writing is the muscular pressure of my finger and thumb, but knowing this does not help anyone to grasp its meaning."[37] And later,

> Penetration to the meaning of a thing or process, as distinct from the ability to describe it exactly, involves a participation by the knower in the known. The meaning of what I am writing is not the physical pressure of thumb and forefinger, or the size of the ink lines with which I form the letters; it is the concepts expressed in the words I am writing. But the only way to understand them is to participate in them—to bring them to life in your own mind by thinking them.[38]

An illiterate person or a person who does not know English will be "a mere onlooker" as modern people are mere onlookers to the universe, seeing only the outward appearances and not the inner meaning that is signified thereby.[39] Hence, the contemporary meaning crisis can be understood as

35. Barfield, "Imagination and Inspiration," in *Rediscovery of Meaning and Other Essays*, 178–79.

36. Blake, "Descriptions of the Last Judgment," in *Complete Poetry and Prose of William Blake*, 566.

37. Barfield, "Rediscovery of Meaning," in *Rediscovery of Meaning and Other Essays*, 14.

38. Barfield, "Rediscovery of Meaning," in *Rediscovery of Meaning and Other Essays*, 14.

39. Barfield, "Rediscovery of Meaning," in *Rediscovery of Meaning and Other Essays*, 24.

a sort of illiteracy in respect to nature. No amount of information about the chemical constitution of the ink, or the physical processes by which the ink was applied, or any other information about the empirically observable page will suffice to grasp the meaning of the text. On the other hand, those who can read English not only *see*, but *see through* the text and participate in Barfield's meaning. In the same way, one who cannot see more than the outsides of nature cannot see the meaning behind or within it.[40] No amount of scientific experiment or examination can help one get at the inside of natural phenomena, where their real significance is revealed.

The significance of the series of events known broadly as the Scientific Revolution is, in Barfield's account, properly understood when considered not merely as an episode in the history of thought, but as a major step in the history of thinking; that is, in the evolution of human consciousness from a state of conscious participation in the life of nature to that of the self-conscious observer.

It is important, again, to emphasize that the change in humanity's perception of the world here described is not, for Barfield, a consequence of correct or erroneous ideas *per se*. This change was, rather, the result of a shift in humanity's consciousness that had been in progress over the course of recorded history. This change in consciousness, he thought, ultimately accounted for the modern crisis of meaning.[41] It is not (or is not primarily) an ideological commitment to scientism, materialism, or any other philosophy that excludes transcendent meaning behind or beyond the appearances of nature that has brought about a diminution of perceived meaning in modern and postmodern consciousness, but the historical development of *a collective habit of inattention* to everything apart from the sort of knowledge referred to in modern times as "scientific." Returning to the distinction Barfield made between the mere appearance of written words and the meaning that they indicate to those who not only *look at*, but *see through* them, into the mind of their author: he compared modern perception of the world to the person who attempts to understand a text by focusing exclusively on the physical causes and effects by which it was produced. Thus, when "investigating the phenomena of nature, exclusive emphasis on physical causes

40. Readers of C. S. Lewis will recognize Barfield's point in the distinction between "looking at" and "looking along" made in the essay "Meditations in a Toolshed," anthologized in *God in the Dock*.

41. Barfield, "Rediscovery of Meaning," in *Rediscovery of Meaning and Other Essays*, 13–14.

and effects involves a corresponding inattention to their meaning."[42] The Scientific Revolution was the historical culmination (though not really the cause) of the diminished experience of meaning, because it was then that "the habit . . . first arose of meticulously observing the facts of nature and systematically interpreting them in terms of physical cause and effect; and this habit has been growing ever since."[43]

Barfield emphasized the point by showing that, though the diminishment of perceived meaning in nature correlates to the rising prominence of scientism, materialism, and other similar views, the crisis of meaning is not limited to those individuals or groups who explicitly affirm such philosophies.[44] Even those who reject materialism on explicitly philosophical grounds, for example, share in certain collective habits of thought that have been acquired through enculturation and the acquisition of language. Thus, even those who ultimately reject scientistic philosophies like materialism, positivism, etc., are inhibited in varying degrees by the limitations of modern consciousness. Barfield explained this in *History, Guilt, and Habit*:

> I can philosophize myself free of philosophical materialism quite easily; and so, I dare say can you. But what we are talking about is *collective* mental habit, which is a very different matter. For that means that, after we have done the philosophizing and gone back to ordinary life, the materialism is still there in our very instruments of thought, and indeed of perception: it signifies that it is there in the meanings of common words we speak and think with . . . it is not merely a habit, but an engrained habit. It is even what we call "common sense."[45]

As stated before, many thinkers have attempted to offer explanations for the meaning crisis. Barfield made a unique contribution to the ongoing conversation by situating it within the context of his theory of the evolution of consciousness. One advantage of this is that it not only gives a compelling explanation of why meaning appears to be absent to many, but also of how those who have lost a sense of meaning might recover it. Insofar as Barfield is right, however, the inability to perceive meaning in the world

42. Barfield, "Rediscovery of Meaning," in *Rediscovery of Meaning and Other Essays*, 14.

43. Barfield, "Rediscovery of Meaning," in *Rediscovery of Meaning and Other Essays*, 13.

44. Barfield, *History, Guilt, and Habit*, 56.

45. Barfield, *History, Guilt, and Habit*, 56.

is historically connected to the rise of modern technology, and the future intellectual integrity and spiritual health of Western culture depends on our ability to overcome the distinctive prejudices of the modern age. This is not to reject science, but scientism; and it is not merely to reject scientism in the intellect, as so many have, but in the imagination as well. Overcoming modern prejudices, Barfield thought, will be the result of intense and receptive study of the past and more resistance to the temptation to view history through modern spectacles. Re-evaluating the modern understanding of nature and the value of technology will require many people to question the assumption that useful beliefs (beliefs, that is, conducive to the manipulation of nature for human purposes) are necessarily true. Even where such beliefs are true, we must not hastily assume that usefulness is a necessary or sufficient condition of truth, or that such truths are in any sense complete. We must be open to believing that there is truth that holds apart from our particular interests and that these truths may be what we are seeking as the meaning of life and the meaning of the universe.

Conclusion

A THINKER OF BARFIELD'S stature deserves a wider audience than he has yet received. We may observe, however, that a river runs deeper, and with greater vigor, where it is narrow; in a similar way, lack of widespread appreciation for Barfield's work has been more than compensated in many cases by the impact it has had on those individuals who have given it due attention. This point, or one much like it, has been a recurring theme in assessments of the reception of Barfield's work, and predictions about its enduring legacy. For instance, Howard Nemerov observed that, though he did not know many poets or teachers who had read *Poetic Diction*, he knew it to be cherished by the few who had: among those who had read it, he said, "it has been valued not only as a secret book, but nearly as a sacred one."[1] And again, regarding *Saving the Appearances,* T. S. Eliot noted that its limited readership was no indication of its quality: as he once wrote in a letter to Barfield, the book was "too profound for our feeble generation of critics."[2] The list of those who have professed this kind of admiration for Barfield, or who have acknowledged a significant intellectual debt to him, includes many other eminent people whose contributions range widely from poetry to theology, and from psychology to physics. In addition to his fellow Inklings, especially Lewis and Tolkien, this list includes (but is not limited to) a diverse set of names like Walter de la Mare, W. H. Auden, Gabriel Marcel, Saul Bellow, Marshall McLuhan, David Bohm, Robert Bly, Richard Wilbur, Harold Bloom, Malcolm Guite, and many others. The historian John Lukacs, speaking about the rise of a certain kind of rigorously historical philosophy,

1. From the foreword to *Poetic Diction*, 1.

2. Eliot's willingness to express his admiration for Barfield is a little surprising since, in print, Barfield had sometimes harshly criticized him and the literary legacy of modernism that was left in his wake (e.g., *Poetic Diction*, 36–37). Nevertheless, Barfield reported being greatly moved when Eliot wrote to him to convey his respect for *Saving the Appearances*. Quoted from Zaleski and Zaleski, *Fellowship*, 439.

said, "Crystalizations of such a philosophy may be found . . . in the writings of Owen Barfield, whom I, together with a scattered minority, consider one of the greatest philosophers in this century."[3] Among this scattered minority is, for instance, the psychologist James Hillman who stated that Barfield is "[o]ne of the most important thinkers of the twentieth century."[4] Though it is not wise to pronounce judgment on the quality of an author's work on the basis of his influence, anyone who wishes to assess Barfield's intellectual legacy should heed the adage to "number not voices, but weigh them."

We wish to note, in conclusion, that the benefits to be derived from serious and sustained attention to Barfield's work extend far beyond merely academic concerns, and moreover, do not depend upon one's acceptance of all or even most of his conclusions. We encourage those who are unable or unwilling to accept Barfield's thesis concerning the evolution of consciousness, with its many historical, philosophical, and theological implications, to look for proof of this benefit in the testimony of Barfield's friends and admirers, many of whom have ultimately rejected much that he said. C. S. Lewis, for instance, serves as a near-perfect model of a largely unconvinced man who nevertheless benefited immensely from a lifetime of critical engagement with Barfield's ideas. As noted before, it is through this engagement that Lewis became aware of his enslavement to the paradigm of materialism, even after he had rejected an overtly materialist philosophy. Relatedly, Barfield opened Lewis's mind by making him aware of his "chronological snobbery." These lessons, being easy to state but hard to really learn, testify to what is perhaps a unique ability of Barfield to teach them. Foremost then, regardless of whether the finer points of his philosophy are judged to be right or wrong, we believe that Barfield's star is on the ascendant and a proper appraisal of his work is only beginning. We hope that this introduction to what Barfield thought may allow more readers to take part in this process.

---

3. Lukacs, *Historical Consciousness*, XXV.
4. See Sherman, *An Ever Diverse Pair.*

Bibliography

Adey, Lionel. *C. S. Lewis' 'Great War' with Owen Barfield*. Victoria, BC: Ink, 2000.

Aquinas, Thomas. *De veritate*. Translated by Robert W. Mulligan. Chicago: Henry Regnery, 1952.

Aristotle. *De Anima* (On the Soul). Translated by J. A. Smith. Internet Classics Archive: http://classics.mit.edu/Aristotle/soul.mb.txt.

———. *Physics*. Translated by S. H. Butcher. Internet Classics Archive: http://classics.mit.edu/Aristotle/poetics.1.1.html.

Bacon, Francis. *The Advancement of Learning*. Edited by Joseph Devey. London: P. F. Collier, 1902. First published 1605.

———. *The New Organon and Other Philosophical Works*. Edited by Lisa Jardine and Michael Silverthorne. Cambridge: Cambridge University Press, 2000. First published 1620.

Barfield, Owen. "Anthroposophy and the Future." https://www.owenbarfield.org/read-online/articles/anthroposophy-and-the-future/.

———. *A Barfield Reader: Selection from the Writings of Owen Barfield*. Edited by G.B. Tennyson. Middletown, CT: Wesleyan University Press, 1999.

———. "Foreword." *VII: Journal of the Marion E Wade Center*, vol. 1, no. 9 (1980).

———. "Greek Thought in English Words." https://www.owenbarfield.org/read-online/articles/greek-thought-in-english-words/.

———. *History in English Words*. Barrington, MA: Lindisfarne, 2003.

———. *History, Guilt, and Habit*. Oxford: Barfield, 2012.

———. "Introducing Rudolf Steiner." *Towards* (Fall-Winter 1983). Reprinted 1995 by the Anthroposophical Society in America.

———. "Owen Barfield and the Origin of Language." https://www.owenbarfield.org/read-online/essays/owen-barfield-and-the-origin-of-language/.

———. *Owen Barfield on C. S. Lewis*. Oxford: Barfield, 2011.

———. *Poetic Diction: A Study in Meaning*. Middletown, CT: Wesleyan University Press, 1973.

———. *The Rediscovery of Meaning and Other Essays*. Oxford: Barfield, 2013.

———. *Romanticism Comes of Age*. Oxford: Barfield, 2012.

———. *Saving the Appearances: A Study in Idolatry*. Middletown, CT: Wesleyan University Press, 1988.

———. *Speaker's Meaning*. Middletown, CT: Wesleyan University Press, 1984.

———. *What Coleridge Thought*. Oxford: Barfield, 2014.

————. *Worlds Apart*. Middletown, CT: Wesleyan University Press, 1963.

Bentham, Jeremy. "Essay on Language." In *The Works of Jeremy Bentham*, vol. VIII, 297–338. London: Simpkin, Marshall, n.d.

Blake, William. *The Complete Poetry and Prose of William Blake*. Edited by David V. Erdman. Oakland, CA: University of California Press, 2008.

Blaxland-de Lange, Simon. *Owen Barfield: Romanticism Come of Age*. 2nd ed. East Sussex: Temple Lodge, 2021.

Boswell, James. *Life of Johnson*. Edited by R. W. Chapman. Oxford: Oxford University Press, 1980.

Carpenter, Humphrey. *The Inklings: C. S. Lewis, J. R. R. Tolkien, Charles Williams and Their Friends*. New York: HarperCollins, 2006.

Chalmers, David. "Facing Up to the Problem of Consciousness," *Journal of Consciousness Studies* vol. 2, no. 3 (1995) 200–219.

Coleridge, Samuel Taylor, *Biographia Literaria*. Edited by Nigel Leask. New York: Everyman Classics, 1997.

Descartes, René. *Passions of the Soul*. Translated by Jonathan Bennett. 2017. https://www.earlymoderntexts.com/assets/pdfs/descartes1649.pdf.

Dewey, John. *Art as Experience*. New York: Penguin, 1934.

Dunning, Stephen. "Charles Williams and Owen Barfield: Common (and Uncommon) Ground." *VII: Journal of the Marion E Wade Center* vol. 21 (2004) 11–30.

Emerson, Ralph Waldo. "Nature." In *The Essential Writings of Ralph Waldo Emerson*, 5–39. New York: Random House, 2000.

Empedocles. *The Fragments of Empedocles*. Translated by William Ellery Leonard. Chicago: The Open Court, 1908.

Flieger, Verlyn. *Splintered Light: Logos and Language in Tolkien's World*. Rev. ed. Kent, OH: Kent State University Press, 2002.

Gadamer, Hans-Georg *Philosophical Hermeneutics*. Translated by D. E. Linge. Oakland, CA: University of California Press, 1976.

————. *Truth and Method*. Translated by Joel Weinsheimer and Donald G. Marshall. New York: Bloomsbury Academic, 2004.

Grefenstette, Jake. "*This Ever Diverse Pair* as an Apology for the Coleridgean Imagination." *Journal of Inklings Studies* vol. 12, no. 1 (April 2022) 60–75.

Gyler, Diana Pavlac. "The Centre of the Inklings: Lewis? Williams? Barfield? Tolkien?" *Mythlore: A Journal of J. R. R. Tolkien, C. S. Lewis, Charles Williams, and Mythopoeic Literature* vol. 26, no. 1 (Fall/Winter 2007) 32.

Haeckel, E. *Riddle of the Universe at the Close of the Nineteenth Century*. Translated by Joseph McCabe. New York: Harper & Brothers, 1905. Project Gutenberg: https://www.gutenberg.org/files/42968/42968-h/42968-h.htm.

Hart, David Bentley. "Concluding Scientific Postscript." In *The New Testament: A Translation*. New Haven: Yale University Press, 2017.

————. "A Reply to N. T. Wright." Eclectic Orthodoxy. https://afkimel.wordpress.com/2018/01/16/a-reply-to-n-t-wright/.

————. "The Spiritual Was More Substantial Than the Material for the Ancients." *Church Life Journal*. https://churchlifejournal.nd.edu/articles/the-spiritual-was-more-substantial-than-the-material-for-the-ancients/.

Harwood, Laurence. *C. S. Lewis, My Godfather*. Downers Grove, IL: InterVarsity, 2007.

Hawking, Stephen. *A Brief History of Time: From the Big Bang to Black Holes*. New York: Bantam, 1988.

Johnson, Samuel. *Lives of Poets: A Selection*. Oxford: Oxford University Press, 2009.

Jung, C. G. *Psychological Types*. The Collected Works of Carl Jung, vol. VI. Princeton: Princeton University Press, 1971.

King, Don. "When Did the Inklings Meet? A Chronological Survey of Their Gatherings: 1933–1954." *Journal of Inklings Studies* 10, no. 2 (2020) 184–204.

Kreeft, Peter. *C. S. Lewis and the Third Millennium: Six Essays on the Abolition of Man*. San Francisco: Ignatius, 1994.

Kuhn, Thomas. *The Structure of Scientific Revolutions*. 4th ed. Chicago: University of Chicago Press, 2017.

Lehrs, Ernst. *Man or Matter: Introduction to a Spiritual Understanding of Nature on the Basis of Goethe's Method of Training Observation and Thought*. London: Faber & Faber, 1958.

Leibniz, Gottfried. *Leibnitz' Monadologie*. Edited by Robert Zimmerman. Vienna: Braumüller und Seidel, 1847.

Levin, Ben, dir. *Owen Barfield: Man and Meaning*. Written and produced by G. B. Tennyson and David Lavery (OwenArts, 1995).

Lewis, C. S. *The Allegory of Love: A Study in Medieval Tradition*. Cambridge: Cambridge University Press, 2013.

———. *All My Roads Before Me: The Diary of C. S. Lewis, 1922–1927*. Edited by Walter Hooper. San Diego: Harcourt, 1991.

———. *The Collected Letters of C. S. Lewis, Vol. 2: Books, Broadcasts, and the War*. Edited by Walter Hooper. New York: Harper Collins, 2004.

———. *The Discarded Image: An Introduction to Medieval and Renaissance Literature*. Cambridge: Canto Classics, 2012.

———. *God in the Dock*. Grand Rapids: Eerdmans, 2014.

———. *Miracles*. In *The Complete C. S. Lewis Signature Classics*. San Francisco: HarperOne, 2002.

———. *Present Concerns*. Edited by Walter Hooper. New York: HarperCollins, 1986.

———. *Selected Literary Essays*. Edited by Walter Hooper. Cambridge: Canto Classics, 2013.

———. *Surprised by Joy: The Shape of My Early Life*. New York: Harcourt, Brace, and World, 1956.

Locke, John. *An Essay Concerning Human Understanding*. 27th ed. London: T. Tegg and Son, 1836.

Loftin, Landon. "Owen Barfield on Science, Technology, and the Modern Crisis of Meaning." *VII: Journal of the Marion E. Wade Center* (2021) 43–58.

Lukacs, John. *Historical Consciousness* or *The Remembered Past*. New York: Schocken, 1985.

MacDonald, George. "The Imagination: Its Function and its Culture." http://www.george-macdonald.com/etexts/the_imagination.html.

MacIntyre, Alasdair. *After Virtue*. New York: Bloomsbury Academic, 2013.

Maximos the Confessor. *On the Cosmic Mystery of Jesus Christ*. Translated by Paul M. Blowers and Robert Louis Wilken. Yonkers, NY: St. Vladimir's Seminary Press, 2003.

Nagel, Thomas. *Mind and Cosmos: Why the Materialist Neo-Darwinian Conception Of Nature Is Almost Certainly False*. Oxford: Oxford University Press, 2012.

Newton, Issac. *The Principia: Mathematical Principles of Natural Philosophy*. Berkeley: University of California Press, 2014. First published 1687.

Plato. *Plato in Twelve Volumes.* Vol. 9. Translated by W. R. M. Lamb. Cambridge: Harvard University Press, 1925.

Plutarch. "De Defectu Oraculorum." *Moralia,* vol. V of the Loeb Classical Library edition. Cambridge: Harvard University Press, 1936.

Reilly, R. J. *Romantic Religion: A Study of Owen Barfield, C. S. Lewis, Charles Williams, and J. R. R. Tolkien.* Barrington, MA: Lindisfarne, 2006.

Russell, Bertrand. *Religion and Science.* Oxford: Oxford University Press, 1935.

Schweitzer, Albert. *Werke aus dem Nachlaß.* Edited by Richard Brüllmann et al. Germany: Verlag C. H. Beck, 1995.

Shakespeare, William. *The Complete Works of William Shakespeare.* Public domain. Available at: http://shakespeare.mit.edu/index.html.

Sherman, Jacob. *An Ever Diverse Pair: Owen Barfield, Teilhard de Chardin and the Evolution of Consciousness.* https://owenbarfield.org/BARFIELD/Barfield_Scholar ship/Sherman/Three.htm.

Steiner, Rudolf. "Awakening to Community." Lecture IV of X. Translated by Marjorie Spock, Stuttgart, February 13, 1923. https://wn.rsarchive.org/Lectures/19230213 p01.html.

———. *Mystics of the Renaissance and Their Relation to Modern Thought.* Translated by Bertram Keightly. London: G. P. Putnam's Sons, 1967.

———. *Philosophy of Freedom.* (GA 4.) Translated by Michael Wilson. London: Rudolf Steiner, 1964. First published in German in 1894.

———. "The Spiritual-Scientific Basis of Goethe's Work." The Rudolf Steiner Research Archive. https://rsarchive.org/Articles/GA035/SSBoGW_index.html.

Tolkien, J. R. R. *The Letters of J. R. R. Tolkien.* Edited by Humphrey Carpenter. New York: Houghton Mifflin Harcourt, 2000.

Thoreau, Henry David. *Walden, Civil Disobedience, and Other Writings.* Edited by William Rossi. The Norton Critical Edition. New York: W. W. Norton, 2008.

Thorson, Stephen. *Joy and Poetic Imagination: Understanding C. S. Lewis's "Great War" with Owen Barfield and Its Significance for Lewis's Conversion and Writings.* Hamden: Winged-Lion 2015.

Treinen, Max Leyf. *The Redemption of Thinking.* Independently published, 2020.

Tylor, Edward B. *Primitive Culture: Researches into the Development of Mythology, Philosophy, Religion, Art, and Custom.* London: Bradbury, Evans, 1871.

Whitehead, A. N. *Science and the Modern World.* New York: Mentor, 1925. 7th printing 1956.

Wittgenstein, Ludwig. *Philosophical Investigations.* Translated by Joachim Schulte and P. M. S. Hacker. Hoboken, NJ: Wiley, 2010.

Zaleski, Carol, and Phillip Zaleski. *The Fellowship: The Literary Lives of the Inklings.* New York: Farrar, Straus and Giroux, 2015.